FRUITS OF THE HEDGEROW

AND

UNUSUAL GARDEN FRUITS

GATHER THEM, COOK THEM, EAT THEM

CHARLOTTE POPESCU

CAVALIER PAPERBACKS

Published by Cavalier Paperbacks 2005
Burnham House,
Upavon,
Wilts SN9 6DU

Website: www.cavalierpaperbacks.co.uk

Cover photo: Charlotte Popescu

ISBN 1-899470-27-1

Printed and bound by The Baskerville Press Ltd.,
Salisbury, Wilts

CONTENTS

GENERAL NOTES

On jellies, jams, butters and cheeses:

For jellies, sugar is generally added in equal amounts to the liquid – so for every 600ml or 1pt of liquid that you produce once you have strained the fruit you should add 450g or 1lb of sugar. The sugar acts as a preservative – you can reduce the amount of sugar added but the preserve will not keep as well. Also you should aim to fill jars to the brim – if not, the extra air in the space at the top of the jar can cause mould to form.

Jams are preserves of whole fruit, or cut up fruit boiled with sugar. Mainly sugar is added in equal quantities to the fruit but if a fruit is low in pectin then often slightly more fruit is used in the recipe than sugar. The addition of lemon juice helps in the natural setting of the fruit. Alternatively you can buy jam sugar which has pectin added. The pectin makes the jam set.

Always allow the sugar to dissolve into your strained fruit over a gentle heat before you bring your preserve to the boil.

For both jellies and jams you should test for a set by placing a little on a cold saucer. If the jelly or jam wrinkles when you push it then it is set. If not, boil for a little longer and test again. Another method you can use is to dip a clean wooden spoon into your mixture to coat it – hold the spoon up over the mixture – if setting point has been reached the preserve will hang on the edge, forming a drop which is reluctant to fall off.

A fruit cheese is made by boiling up sieved fruit pulp, for example from damsons, quinces or apples with an equal amount of sugar until the mixture has a very thick consistency. It should be stored in small moulds, turned out and cut up like a slice of cheese to eat with meat or on bread and butter.

A fruit butter is more spreadable than a cheese and has a lower proportion of sugar to fruit pulp so does not keep as long as a fruit cheese. It can be used as a filling for sponges.

Yield, especially when making jellies, is often difficult to predict because much depends on the juiciness of the fruit. The amount of sugar added will determine the amount of jelly you can expect - 900g, 2lb of sugar should maked 1.5kg, 3lb 5oz of jelly.

BILBERRIES

Bilberries are similar to blueberries and can be found mainly in the North of England and Scotland on heaths and moorlands but also in the West. They are small bluish-black berries and are also known as whinberries or whortleberries. Being so small they are difficult and time consuming to pick and you should beware because they will stain your hands purple. Bilberries are rich in Vitamin A and potassium.

BILBERRY KISSEL
Serves 6

1kg, 2.2lb bilberries
50g, 2oz granulated sugar
4 tbsp honey
2 tbsp orange juice + 4 tbsp water
3 tbsp wholemeal flour

Put the bilberries, sugar, honey, orange juice and water into a saucepan, cover and cook gently for 15 minutes, stirring to dissolve the sugar. Mix a little of the juice into the flour to make a paste. Pour this into the fruit and stir until the sauce thickens. Cool and serve with ice cream or yoghurt.

BILBERRY BRANDY

1kg, 2.2lb bilberries
175g, 6oz granulated sugar
¼ tsp ground ginger
1 x 70cl bottle of brandy

Purée the bilberries and mix with the sugar and ginger. Put into a Kilner jar and fill up with the brandy. Keep covered and in the dark for 2 months, stirring the mixture every week. Let it remain unstirred for a further month and then strain into a clean bottle. Use the brandy soaked bilberries to eat with ice cream.

BILBERRY SORBET
Serves 4

450g, 1lb bilberries
150ml, ¼pt water
100g, 4oz granulated sugar
juice of 1 lemon
1 egg white

Put the bilberries in a saucepan with the water and gently heat until they become soft and juicy. Sieve the fruit and transfer the juice to a saucepan. Add the sugar. Bring the juice to the boil and boil for 3 minutes. Allow to cool and stir in the lemon juice. Freeze to the slushy stage. Whisk the mixture to break down any ice crystals. Whisk the egg white and gently fold this into the sorbet. Freeze again until firm.

BILBERRY JAM
Makes 1.5kg, 3½lb

1kg, 2.2lb bilberries
1kg, 2.2lb granulated sugar
2 tbsp water

Put the bilberries in a saucepan with the water and cook gently until the juices run and the fruit softens. Add the sugar and bring to the boil. Boil until setting point is reached – this will not take long as bilberries, especially slightly under-ripe ones, contain a good amount of pectin.

BLACKBERRIES

Blackberries or brambles are widespread in hedgerows and are the most commonly used wild fruits. They have been found in many of the earliest areas of habitation and were well known to the Greeks, who used the leaves for their herbal properties as well as the fruit. There is evidence that blackberries were eaten in England in Neolithic times because pips have been found in the stomach contents of a Stone Age man found preserved in clay along the Essex coast.

There are many different varieties (there being no single native blackberry) which are referred to as hybrids and you can notice a difference in each blackberry bush if you look carefully at the fruits or the flowers. In fact there are over 2,000 microspecies of wild blackberry. The reason for this is that they cross-pollinate very easily and birds spread the seeds in their droppings. The bushes spread very effectively because, as their tips bend towards the earth, they form roots.

The dewberry is a distinct species which has smaller fruit than blackberries. These also mature earlier than most blackberries and have a matt rather than a glossy finish. Cloudberries are also closely related to blackberries but in this country are only found in Scotland.

Folklore tells us that it is unlucky to eat blackberries after 29 September (Michaelmas Day) as it is said that the devil has spat on them. In fact this date becomes 10 October in our modern calendar. This is about the time that blackberries start being past their best and

become watery and tasteless. However although traditionally one picks blackberries from mid August in some areas they are now becoming ripe in July. The lowest berry in each cluster, the one at the tip of the stalk ripens first and this is the sweetest and most succulent. After a couple of weeks the other berries will ripen but these tend to be less juicy.

Blackberries are a versatile fruit that can be mixed with other fruits and are especially good with apples. Wild blackberries tend to be pippy so you may wish to purée and sieve them before use or make blackberry jelly.

Blackberries were in the past well known as a fruit to be eaten to help prevent scurvy. They are high in fibre and contain a wealth of minerals, including magnesium, iron and calcium. They are rich in vitamin C, potassium and are a low fat source of vitamin E. They also contain bioflavonoids which act like antioxidants, protecting against cell damage.

The following recipe is useful as a basis for puddings.

APPLE AND BLACKBERRY PURÉE

450g, 1lb cooking apples, peeled, cored and sliced
225g, 8oz blackberries
100g, 4oz granulated sugar

Combine the apples, blackberries and granulated sugar in a saucepan and cover. You shouldn't need to add any water as the blackberries will produce plenty of juice. Cook gently for about 20 minutes. Sieve the mixture to remove the blackberry pips.

11

BLACKBERRY AND APPLE AMBER
Serves 6

225g, 8oz shortcrust pastry
450g, 1lb cooking apples, peeled, cored and chopped
100g, 4oz blackberries
juice of 1 lemon
100g, 4oz brown sugar
2 eggs, separated
100g, 4oz caster sugar

Roll out the pastry and use to line a greased 20cm, 8in flan dish. Prick and bake blind in the oven at gas mark 5, 190°C (375°F) for 15 minutes. Cook the apples and blackberries with the lemon juice and brown sugar over a gentle heat for 15 minutes. Sieve the apple and blackberry mixture and when slightly cooled mix in the egg yolks. Spread over the pastry base. Whisk the egg whites until stiff and whisk in the sugar bit by bit until the meringue is thick and glossy. Spread over the blackberry and apple. Bake in the oven at gas mark 3, 160°C (325°F) for a further 40 minutes, by which time the meringue will be golden and crisp on top but soft inside. Serve with cream.

PEAR AND BLACKBERRY PAVLOVA

Serves 6 – 8

For the pavlova
4 egg whites
225g, 8oz caster sugar
½ tbsp cornflour, sifted
1 tsp white wine vinegar
1 tsp vanilla essence

For the topping
150ml, ¼pt whipping cream
150ml, ¼pt soured cream
225g, 8oz pears, peeled, cored and sliced
225g, 8oz blackberries
50g, 2oz granulated sugar

To make the pavlova, beat the egg whites until stiff. Gradually beat in the caster sugar, a little at a time. Sprinkle the cornflour, vinegar and vanilla over the mixture and fold in carefully. Make a circle with the meringue mixture on a large greased baking sheet. Bake for an hour at gas mark 1, 120°C (275°F). The pavlova should be crisp on the outside with a soft marshmallow centre. Whip the cream with the soured cream. Spread this over the meringue. Cook the blackberries with the granulated sugar over a gentle heat until the juices run. Add the pears and cook for a couple more minutes. Carefully pour the pear slices and blackberries over the cream and serve at once.

BLACKBERRY AND ELDERFLOWER FOOL
Serves 4

225g, 8oz blackberries
60ml, 2fl oz elderflower cordial
150ml, ¼pt double cream
2 egg whites

Cook the blackberries in the elderflower cordial in a covered saucepan for about 15 minutes, or until the berries are tender. Remove the lid and boil rapidly to reduce the liquid a little. Sieve the fruit and cool. Whip the double cream until thick and carefully fold into the fruit mixture. Lastly whisk the egg whites until thick and fold them into the fruit as well.

BRAMBLE MOUSSE
Serves 6 – 8

450g, 1lb blackberries
juice of 1 lemon
3 eggs, separated
175g, 6oz caster sugar
25g, 1oz gelatine
300ml, ½pt double cream, whipped

Cook the blackberries in the lemon juice in a saucepan with a tightly fitting lid. When the brambles have softened, remove from the heat, sieve them and allow to cool. Put 3 tablespoons of water in a small saucepan and sprinkle in the gelatine. Leave to soften a little and then heat very gently until the gelatine has dissolved. Leave to cool. Whisk the egg yolks and gradually add the caster sugar, whisking until you have a thick, pale mixture. Stir in the cooled blackberry mixture and the gelatine. Add the whipped cream and lastly whisk the egg whites until stiff and fold them in too. Pour the mousse into a bowl and leave to set.

APPLE AND BLACKBERRY HOT SOUFFLÉS
Serves 6

These soufflés are low fat.

300ml, ½pt apple and blackberry purée
75g, 3oz caster sugar
3 egg whites

Butter six 150ml, ¼pt small pudding basins or mini soufflé dishes. Put a small spoonful of blackberry and apple purée in the bottom of each one. Whisk the egg whites until stiff and whisk in the caster sugar. Fold the purée into this meringue mixture until evenly combined. Spoon equal amounts into the pudding basins. Pop in the oven at gas mark 6, 200°C (400°F) on preheated baking sheets for 10 minutes. Serve immediately, dusted with icing sugar if liked.

BLACKBERRY SNOW
Serves 4

450g, 1lb blackberries
2 egg whites
100g, 4oz caster sugar
300ml, ½pt double cream

Rub the blackberries through a sieve to form a purée, pour into a container and freeze for 2 hours. Whisk the egg whites until stiff and gradually add the sugar while continuing to whisk. Take the blackberry purée from the freezer and mash to break down any large ice

crystals. Fold the cream and egg white mixture together and fold into the semi-frozen blackberry purée to give a swirled effect. Spoon into glasses or into a serving bowl and serve immediately.

BLACKBERRY ICE CREAM
Serves 4 – 6

450g, 1lb blackberries, puréed and sieved
75g, 3oz icing sugar
Squeeze of lemon juice
75g, 3oz granulated sugar
120ml, 4 fl oz water
3 egg yolks
300ml, ½pt double cream, whipped

Put the blackberry purée in a bowl with the icing sugar and a squeeze of lemon juice. Dissolve the sugar with the water in a heavy-based saucepan and boil for 5 minutes. Whisk the egg yolks until thick and then whisk in the boiling syrup. Continue to whisk until the mixture cools and thickens again. Fold in the blackberry purée and cream. Spoon into a freezer container and freeze until firm.

ICED BLACKBERRY AND APPLE SOUFFLÉ
Serves 6

2 tbsp sloe gin
300ml, ½pt apple and blackberry purée (see page11)
150g, 5oz granulated sugar
120ml, 4fl oz water
3 egg whites
150ml, ¼pt double cream, whipped

Stir the sloe gin into the purée. Dissolve the sugar in the water and boil for 5 minutes. In the meantime whisk the egg whites until stiff and when the sugar syrup is ready whisk it into the egg whites. Fold the purée and cream into egg white mixture and when all is thoroughly combined transfer to a freezer container and freeze until firm.

BLACKBERRY AND LIME SORBET
Serves 4

300ml, ½pt water
175g, 6oz granulated sugar
juice of 1 lime
450g, 1lb blackberries
2 egg whites

Put the water and sugar in a saucepan and heat gently until the sugar has dissolved. Bring to the boil and boil for 5 minutes until syrupy. Remove from the heat, stir in the lime juice and leave to cool. Meanwhile put the blackberries in a saucepan and heat gently until the juices start to run which should be after about 5

minutes. Sieve the blackberries and stir the purée into the cooled syrup. Freeze to the slushy stage. Whisk the mixture to break down any ice crystals. Whisk the egg whites until stiff and fold these into the blackberry mixture. Freeze until firm.

BLACKBERRY AND REDCURRANT SORBET
Serves 6 – 8

450g, 1lb blackberries
450g, 1lb redcurrants
225g, 8oz granulated sugar
juice of 1 lemon
1 egg white

Put the blackberries and redcurrants together in a saucepan with a couple of tablespoons of water and gently heat them until they become soft and juicy. Sieve the fruit and you should end up with about 600ml, 1pt of juice. Transfer to a saucepan and add the sugar. Bring the juice to the boil and boil for 3 minutes. Allow to cool and stir in the lemon juice. Freeze to the slushy stage. Whisk the mixture to break down any ice crystals. Whisk the egg white and gently fold this into the sorbet. Freeze again until firm.

BLACKBERRY LIQUEUR – MURE

450g, 1lb blackberries
1 x 750ml, 1¼pt bottle of brandy
75g, 3oz granulated sugar
stick of cinnamon
3 cloves

Whiz up the blackberries, brandy and granulated sugar in a food processor. Pour into a bottle, add the cinnamon and cloves, cork and leave for 2 months. Strain and transfer to sterilised bottles. This can be used like cassis, added to wine to make a kir or to champagne to make kir royale.

BLACKBERRY CORDIAL

450g, 1lb blackberries
100g, 4oz granulated sugar
600ml, 1pt sweet cider
2 tbsp honey

Purée the blackberries with the granulated sugar. Add to the cider and mix in the honey. Put in a Kilner jar and seal down. Leave for 6 months. Then strain the liquid through muslin and bottle. If you can, wait another month before drinking. Dilute for a refreshing drink.

BLACKBERRY VODKA

450g, 1lb blackberries
225g, 8oz granulated sugar
750ml, 1¼pts vodka

Put the blackberries in a Kilner jar in layers with the sugar. Pour on the vodka, cover and shake. Put the jar in a cool, dark place for 3 months, shaking every couple of weeks. Strain off the blackberries and pour the liqueur into a bottle.

BLACKBERRY KETCHUP

This goes well with cold meats.

1.35kg, 3lb blackberries
water
granulated sugar
½ tsp dry mustard
2 tsp ground ginger
pinch of ground cloves
600ml, 1pt vinegar

Put the blackberries in a saucepan, with enough water to come halfway up, and cook until soft. Sieve them and measure the purée. For every 600ml, 1pt you will need 100g, 4oz of sugar. Pour the blackberry purée into a large saucepan; add the sugar, mustard powder, ginger, ground cloves and vinegar. Simmer gently to dissolve the sugar and continue to cook for about 30 minutes by which time the mixture should be thick. Pour into small bottles and seal tightly.

BLACKBERRY AND APPLE JELLY
Makes about 4kg, 9lb

1kg, 2.2lb cooking apples, peeled, cored and sliced
1kg, 2.2lb blackberries
water
granulated sugar
juice of ½ a lemon

Cook the blackberries and apples together with enough water to just cover the fruit. When soft pour into muslin and suspend over a large bowl. Allow to drip through the muslin overnight and squeeze as much liquid out of the muslin as you can the next day so that you are left with just a mush of blackberry pips. Pour the juice into a large saucepan and add the sugar and lemon juice. For every 600ml or 1pt of juice you need 450g, 1lb of sugar. Boil rapidly until set. You can test for a set by dropping a little of the hot liquid onto a saucer. If it appears jelly-like, it is set. Pour into warmed jars and seal.

BLACKBERRY, APPLE AND
CARDAMOM JAM
Makes 1kg, 2.2lb

450g, 1lb cooking apples, weight when peeled, cored
and diced
150ml, ¼pt water
900g, 2lb blackberries, puréed and sieved
675g, 1½lb granulated sugar

3 cardamom pods, seeds lightly crushed
juice of ½ a lemon

Put the apples in a large saucepan with the water, bring to the boil and simmer for 15 minutes. Add the blackberry purée and cook for a further 5 minutes. Add the sugar, cardamom seeds, wrapped in a piece of muslin and the lemon juice. Heat gently while the sugar dissolves, then boil for about 20 minutes until the jam is set. Pot and seal.

BLACKBERRY AND APPLE CURD
Makes 450g, 1lb

175g, 6oz blackberries
1 cooking apple, peeled, cored and sliced
juice of ½ a lemon
50g, 2oz butter
225g, 8oz granulated sugar
2 eggs

Put the blackberries and sliced apple in a saucepan and gently heat until the juices run and the fruit is soft. Sieve and put the fruit purée in a bowl above a pan of simmering water with the lemon juice, butter and sugar. Stir until the butter melts and the sugar dissolves. Beat the eggs and stir into the fruit mixture. Cook gently until the curd thickens. Strain through a sieve and spoon into a clean, warm jar. This curd does not keep for more than a couple of weeks. Use it on toast, to fill a sponge cake or as a topping for ice cream.

CRAB APPLES

Crab apple trees are widespread in the countryside in woods, hedgerows, on heaths and on roadside verges. The apples are round, yellowish green, sometimes turning bright red and can be picked from July to December. Wild crab apples are the origin of all our cultivated apples. There are also large numbers of domestic apples that have seeded themselves in the wild (often from discarded apple cores) and have reverted to a wild form or crossed with real crab apple trees.

Wild apple trees, often found on roadsides, bear fruit which is quite edible raw although often quite sharp in flavour. Crab apples cannot usually be eaten raw but make a very good jelly since they have a high pectin content and work well added to other fruits. One well known variety, worth growing in your garden, 'John Downie' has orange, conical shaped fruit sweet enough to be eaten raw. There are also dwarf varieties available such as 'Laura' which can be grown in large pots as they only grow to about 1.8m, 6ft.

Crab apple trees are worth growing in your garden because they are good pollinators of domestic apples trees, are self fertile, hardy and produce lovely blossom in the spring.

The Indians in North America found crab apples so sour they used to gather them during the autumn and bury them in the ground until spring. They were supposed to be sweeter after they had been dug up. Crab apples were once used to make verjuice, an acid liquor which was used in cooking.

SPICED CRAB APPLES

750ml, 1¼pt white wine vinegar
1 x 7.5cm, 3in cinnamon stick
10 cloves
5 black peppercorns
1.35kg, 3lb crab apples
800g, 1¾lb granulated sugar

Put the vinegar and spices into a pan and bring to the boil. Simmer for 5 minutes. Strain and add the crab apples. Simmer gently in the hot vinegar until just tender. Remove the apples with a slotted spoon and transfer to hot jars. Add the sugar to the vinegar and gently heat until it dissolves. Then boil rapidly until syrupy. Pour the vinegar syrup over the apples, making sure the crab apples are covered. Seal and store.

CRAB APPLE JELLY

Yield will vary depending on the juiciness of the fruit - 1kg or 2lb of sugar should yield 1.5kg or just over 3lb of jelly.

1.35kg, 3lb crab apples
water
granulated sugar

Put the crab apples in a saucepan with just enough water to cover them. Cook until soft and then strain through muslin overnight. Try not to squeeze the bag or the jelly will be cloudy. Measure the liquid and allow 450g, 1lb of sugar for 600ml, 1pt of juice. Return to the saucepan with the sugar and lemon juice. Heat gently to dissolve the sugar and then boil until setting point is reached. Pour into warmed, sterilised jars and seal.

CRAB APPLE AND DAMSON JELLY

Yield will vary as in the previous recipe.

1.35kg, 3lb crab apples
1kg, 2.2lb damsons
water
granulated sugar
juice of 1 lemon

Halve the apples and put in a preserving pan with the damsons and water to cover. Cook until the fruits are soft – probably about 40 minutes. Strain through muslin

overnight. Measure the liquid and allow 450g, 1lb of sugar for every 600ml or 1pt of juice. Return to the saucepan with the sugar and lemon juice. Heat gently to dissolve the sugar and then boil until setting point is reached. Pour into warmed, sterilised jars and seal.

CRAB APPLE BUTTER

900g, 2lb crab apples
600ml, 1pt water
granulated sugar
clear honey
½ tsp ground nutmeg
¼ tsp mixed spice
¼ tsp cinnamon

Halve the crab apples if they are large and put in a saucepan with the water. Simmer gently until they are soft and then sieve the apples to give a smooth purée. Measure this and to each 600ml, 1pt of purée add 350g, 12oz sugar and 100g, 4oz of honey. Put the purée, sugar and honey in a saucepan with the spices and stir over a low heat until the sugar has dissolved. Simmer until the mixture is thick. Transfer to moulds and cover.

CRAB APPLE CREAM ICE
Serves 4 – 6

1kg, 2.2lb crab apples
350g, 12oz granulated sugar
juice of 1 orange
300ml, ½pt whipping cream

Cut the crab apples in half and put them in a large saucepan with enough water just to cover them. Simmer until soft and then pass through a sieve. Dissolve the granulated sugar in 150ml, ¼pt of water and boil for 5 minutes. Allow to cool and then stir into the apple purée along with the orange juice. Freeze until the slushy stage and then beat well. Fold the cream into the half frozen mixture and freeze again until firm.

APPLE AND GINGER JAM
Makes 2.25kg, 5lb

1.35kg, 3lb wild or cooking apples, chopped
1.35kg, 3lb granulated sugar
peel from 2 lemons
25g, 1oz root ginger
50g, 2oz stem ginger, chopped

Put the chopped apples in a saucepan with the water and simmer for 15 minutes or until softened. Sieve the apples to remove the pips and peel. Return to the saucepan and add the sugar. Peel the ginger and put in a muslin bag with the lemon peel before adding to the pan. Heat until the sugar has dissolved and cook until setting point is reached. Stir in the chopped stem ginger, pour into warmed jars and seal.

DAMSONS AND BULLACES

Damsons came from Damascus originally and were found there by the Crusaders in the 12th century. It is thought that the Duke of Anjou brought them back to Europe after a pilgrimage to Jerusalem. Damsons are larger than bullaces with an oval shape and blue-black fruit. The flesh is greeny yellow.

Bullaces are the wild ancestors of plums and are native to Europe and Asia. They were grown by the Romans and Anglo Saxons and were popular in medieval orchards. The bullace makes a large bush or small tree which has some thorns but less than you would find on a sloe bush. The bluey black bullaces known as Black Bullaces are similar to sloes but slightly larger. There are also greeny yellow ones, known as Shepherd's Bullaces. The fruits are round and very bitter like sloes and so are not usually eaten raw. The flesh is yellow. A third variety, White Bullace has small, flattened fruits and a yellow skin mottled with red – these are sweeter than the other types. Bullaces ripen later than damsons in November. They grow in hedgerows and on the edges of woods.

Both damsons and bullaces are, like plums, high in potassium, a good source of vitamin A and contain small amounts of calcium and magnesium.

DAMSON AND BRAMBLE FOOL
Serves 6 – 8

900g, 2lb damsons
100g, 4oz granulated sugar
150ml, ¼pt double cream, whipped
150ml, ¼pt mascarpone
2 egg whites
100g, 4oz blackberries, sieved

Cook the damsons with the granulated sugar in a little water for 10 minutes. Discard the stones and purée the flesh. Mix with the whipped cream and mascarpone. Whisk the egg whites until fairly stiff and fold into the mixture. Divide between individual dishes and swirl a little of the sieved blackberries over each dish.

DAMSON SYLLABUB
Serves 4

450g, 1lb damsons, halved and stoned
100g, 4oz caster sugar
150ml, ¼pt water
2 tbsp brandy
2 egg whites
300ml, ½pt double cream, whipped

Place the damsons in a saucepan with the sugar and water. Heat gently and simmer until soft. Rub the fruit through a sieve. When cold stir in the brandy. Whisk the egg whites until stiff and fold into the damson purée with the cream. Turn into glasses or a bowl.

DAMSON, APPLE AND BLACKBERRY
SUMMER PUDDING
Serves 4 – 6

450g, 1lb damsons, stoned
225g, 8oz cooking apples, peeled, cored and sliced
225g, 8oz blackberries
175g, 6oz granulated sugar
150ml, ¼pt water
10 slices of brown bread, crusts removed

Cook the damsons, apples and blackberries together with the sugar and water until tender. Line the bottom and sides of a 1.1litre, 2pt pudding basin with the bread. Reserve a little of the juice from the fruit. Pour the stewed fruit into the basin and top with a slice of bread to make a lid. Put a plate on top of the basin and weight it down. Chill the pudding overnight. Turn out on to a serving dish. Pour the reserved juice over the top to conceal any brown bits of bread. Serve with cream.

DAMSON AND GINGER MOUSSE
Serves 4

450g, 1lb damsons
2 balls of stem ginger, chopped
2 tbsp granulated sugar
3 tsp gelatine
300ml, ½pt whipping cream
2 egg whites

Stew the damsons in a little water. Discard the stones and purée the flesh. Stir in the ginger and sugar. In a small bowl sprinkle the gelatine over 150ml, ¼pt of water. Place the bowl over a pan of hot water and stir until dissolved. Stir into the warm damson purée. Allow to cool slightly. Whip the cream. Whisk the egg whites until stiff. Fold the cream and then the egg whites into the damson mixture. Turn into a serving bowl and leave to set in the fridge.

DAMSON AND PEAR CRUMBLE
Serves 4

450g, 1lb damsons, halved and stoned
2 pears, cored, sliced and chopped
1 tbsp grated orange rind
50g, 2oz granulated sugar

Topping
100g, 4oz plain flour
½ tsp cinnamon
75g, 3oz margarine

75g, 3oz demerara sugar
40g, 1½oz porridge oats

Put the damsons and pears in a pie dish with the grated rind and granulated sugar. Make the crumble topping by rubbing the margarine into the flour and cinnamon. Stir in the demerara sugar and oats. Spread over the fruit mixture and bake in the oven at gas mark 5, 190°C (375°F) for 30 minutes.

DAMSON ICE CREAM
Serves 6 – 8

1kg, 2.2lb damsons
150ml, ¼pt red wine
75g, 3oz caster sugar
2 tbsp lemon juice
4 egg yolks
450ml, ¾pt single cream

Poach the damsons in the wine and 50g, 2oz of the sugar for 15 minutes. Strain and reserve the liquid. Remove the stones from the damsons, purée the flesh and pass through a sieve. Stir in the lemon juice. Whisk the egg yolks with the remaining sugar until thick and light. Heat the cream until just below boiling point. Pour the hot cream on to the egg yolks, whisking continuously. Heat gently, stirring all the time but do not let the custard boil. When it is thick, remove from the heat and cool slightly. Mix in the damson purée and cool completely before pouring into a freezer container and freezing until firm, beating twice at hourly intervals. Put the reserved juice into a saucepan and boil to reduce it by half. Serve this damson sauce with the ice cream.

ICED DAMSON SOUFFLÉ
Serves 6

450g, 1lb damsons, halved and stoned
60ml, 2fl oz water
2 tbsp sloe gin
3 egg whites
175g, 6oz caster sugar
300ml, ½pt double cream

Cook the damsons in the water and then purée them. Stir in the sloe gin. Whisk the egg whites until stiff and gradually whisk in the caster sugar. Fold the damson purée into this meringue mixture. Add the double cream and when all is thoroughly combined, transfer to a freezer container and freeze until firm.

DAMSON AND APPLE JELLY

Yield will vary depending on the juiciness of the fruit - 1kg or 2lb of sugar should yield 1.5kg or just over 3lb of jelly.

1kg, 2.2lb cooking apples, unpeeled and uncored
1kg, 2.2lb damsons
1.2 litres, 2 pts water
granulated sugar

Cut up the apples and put into a large preserving pan with the damsons and water. Boil until the fruit is soft and then strain through a muslin bag. Weigh the juice and allow 450g, 1lb of sugar for every 600ml or 1pt of

juice. Gently heat the juice and sugar until the sugar has dissolved and then boil rapidly until setting point is reached. There is no need for the addition of lemon juice as the apples are high in pectin. Pour into warmed, sterilised jars and seal. This makes a clear jelly.

DAMSON JAM
Makes about 2kg, 4½lb

1kg, 2.2lb damsons
450ml, ¾pt water
1.35kg, 3lb granulated sugar
juice of 1 lemon

Wash the damsons and place in a large saucepan with the water. Bring to the boil and then reduce the heat and simmer for about 30 minutes. Add the granulated sugar and allow to dissolve. Pour in the lemon juice and bring to the boil. Boil rapidly until setting point is reached – this should take about 20 minutes. Skim off any scum and remove all the damson stones with a slotted spoon. Spoon into warmed jars and seal.

DAMSON AND BLACKBERRY JAM
Makes about 2kg, 4.4lb

900g, 2lb damsons, halved and stoned
350g, 12oz blackberries
1.35kg, 3lb granulated sugar
1 tbsp lemon juice
knob of butter

Put the damson and blackberries in a preserving pan and simmer gently for about 20 minutes. Then add the sugar and lemon juice and stir until the sugar has dissolved. Add the butter and bring the mixture to a boil. Boil fast until setting point is reached. Remove the pan from the heat and cool a little before pouring into warm jars.

DAMSON CHEESE
Should make about 1.35kg, 3lb of cheese

1.35kg, 3lb damsons
1kg, 2.2lb light brown sugar

Put the damsons in a large pan with just enough water to prevent burning. Cook until very soft. Sieve to remove stones and skin and return the fruit pulp to the pan. Add the sugar which should be about three quarters of the weight of the fruit pulp. Heat gently and cook until the mixture is very thick and drawing a spoon through it leaves a deep channel. Cooking time may be up to an hour depending on the moisture content of the fruit. Put into oiled containers and seal. This cheese is best left for a couple of months for the flavour to mature.

DAMSON CHUTNEY
Makes 2.25kg, 5lb

450g, 1lb onions, peeled and chopped
1 clove of garlic, peeled and chopped
600ml, 1pt white malt vinegar
1 tsp mustard powder
1 tsp ground ginger
½ tsp ground nutmeg
450g, 1lb peeled, cored and chopped cooking apples
1.35kg, 3lb damsons, halved and stoned
450g, 1lb granulated sugar

Put the onion and garlic in a preserving pan with half the vinegar and the spices. Simmer for 15 minutes. Add the chopped apples with the damsons and remaining vinegar. Simmer for 30 minutes and then add the sugar and stir over a low heat to dissolve. Raise the heat slightly and simmer until thick. Spoon into warm jars and seal.

BULLACE AND PEAR JAM
Makes about 4.5kg, 10lb

1.35kg, 3lb pears, peeled and diced
1.35kg, 3lb bullaces, stones removed
600ml, 1pt water
juice from 1 lemon
2.7kg, 6lb granulated sugar

Place the fruit and water in a large preserving pan and bring to the boil. Simmer gently until the fruit are soft. Add the lemon juice and sugar and stir until the sugar has dissolved. Bring to the boil and boil rapidly until setting point is reached. Pour into warmed jars and seal.

BULLACE AND QUINCE JELLY

Yield will vary depending on the juiciness of the fruit - 1kg or 2lb of sugar should yield 1.5kg or just over 3lb of jelly.

1kg, 2.2lb bullaces
1kg, 2.2lb quinces, unpeeled, chopped
1.5 litres, 3pts water
2 tbsp lemon juice
granulated sugar

Put the bullaces and quinces, including the pips, in a preserving pan with the water and cook until soft. This will probably take at least 30 minutes. Strain through muslin and measure the liquid. For every 600ml or 1pt of juice add 450g or 1lb of sugar. Return the liquid to

the pan and add the sugar and lemon juice. You can omit the lemon juice if the quinces are unripe as they will probably contain enough pectin. Heat gently until the sugar has dissolved. Boil until setting point is reached. Pour into warmed jars and seal.

BULLACE RELISH
Makes about 1kg, 2lb

675g, 1½lb bullaces, halved and stoned
225g, 8oz cooking apples, peeled, cored and diced
225g, 8oz onions, peeled and minced
100g, 4oz carrots, peeled and diced
300ml, ½pt cider vinegar
225g, 8oz brown sugar
½ tsp cinnamon
½ tsp ground ginger
½ tsp nutmeg
½ tsp ground cloves
2 tsp salt

Put the bullaces, apples, onions and carrots in a large saucepan with half the vinegar and simmer for about 40 minutes until the fruit is soft. Add the rest of the vinegar with the sugar, spices and salt. Continue cooking, stirring every so often, until the relish is thick. This should take about an hour. Pour into warm jars and seal.

ELDERBERRIES & ELDERFLOWERS

When the elder is white, brew and bake a peck,
When the elder is black, brew and bake a sack

You may shear your sheep,
When the elder blossoms peep

The elder is native to Britain, Europe and Scandinavia. It is thought the Romans may have imported the elder to Britain. The plant has been highly regarded for centuries as it has so many uses. The wood was used in the past for making musical instruments. The elder was regarded as a sacred tree and people believed they would be cured if they cut down or destroyed an elder. This old belief originated from Judas, the Apostle who was said to have hanged himself on a cross made from an elder tree. Those who gather firewood and are in the know, avoid elder for burning, not because it burns badly, but because to burn it is to ' raise the devil.'

Widespread in hedgerows, woods and on roadside verges the elder is a tall, fast growing shrub which has a dual purpose. The elderflowers appear in June and the berries in September. Elderflowers make a great cordial and work well with gooseberries. They also add flavour to strawberries and other fruits. Don't wash the elderflowers as this will destroy their flavour. The flowers are also useful commercially as an ingredient in skin creams and eye lotions. Elderberries are small and black and grow in large, umbrella like clusters which droop down as the fruits ripen. They should be picked as soon as the berries turn black but used straightaway as they do not keep. Elderberries are very rich in vitamin C and are rich in minerals. They have a flavour similar to blackcurrants.

ELDERFLOWER CORDIAL

This is a great drink to make in June when the elderflowers are in season.

1. 3litres, 2½ pts water
1.8kg, 4 lb granulated sugar
25 elderflower heads
2 lemons, sliced
65g, 2½oz citric acid
¼ Campden tablet (can be bought from brewing and wine making suppliers)

Place the water and granulated sugar in a large saucepan and bring to the boil gradually to dissolve the sugar. Remove from the heat. Place the elderflowers, slices of lemon and citric acid in a large plastic container and pour over the sugar syrup. Cover and leave to infuse for three days, stirring once a day. Strain through muslin over a colander. If you want the cordial to keep for up to a year add a quarter of a Campden tablet dissolved in a tablespoon of water to the strained syrup. Pour into sterilised bottles and store.

ELDERFLOWER FRITTERS
Makes 10 fritters

100g, 4oz plain flour
2 small eggs
300ml, ½pt milk
10 small elderflower heads
caster sugar and lemon for serving
sunflower oil for deep frying

Make up the batter by whizzing together the flour, eggs and milk in a food processor. Wash and trim the elderflower heads leaving a stalk so that you can dip them in the batter. Heat the oil in a frying pan and fry the fritters using the stalk to remove each one when it is golden brown. Trim off the stalks and serve with caster sugar and lemon.

ELDERFLOWER CREAM WITH RASPBERRY AND PEAR COMPOTE
Serves 4

25g, 1oz granulated sugar
6 heads of fresh elderflowers
150ml, ¼pt mascarpone
450g, 1lb pears, peeled, cored and chopped
450g, 1lb raspberries
300ml, ½pt apple juice
1 cinnamon stick
2 strips of lemon rind

First make the elderflower cream. Put the granulated sugar and 150ml, ¼pt of water in a saucepan and heat gently to dissolve the sugar. Then boil rapidly to reduce the liquid by half. Remove from the heat and add the elderflowers. Leave to infuse for at least an hour. Then strain the syrup and fold in the mascarpone. Put the pears in a saucepan with the apple juice, cinnamon stick and lemon rind and simmer for 10 minutes until the pears have softened. Add the raspberries and simmer for another 5 minutes. Remove the cinnamon stick and lemon rind and serve warm with the elderflower cream.

ELDERFLOWER SORBET
Serves 3 - 4

300ml, ½pt water
75g, 3oz granulated sugar
strip of lemon rind + juice of 1 lemon
25g, 1oz elderflowers
1 egg white

Put the water, granulated sugar and the strip of lemon rind in a saucepan and heat gently until the sugar has dissolved. Bring to the boil and then simmer for 5 minutes. Allow to cool and add the lemon juice and elderflowers. Leave to infuse for at least 30 minutes. Strain the liquid and freeze to the slushy stage, then remove and beat. Beat the egg white and whisk into the half frozen sorbet. Return to the freezer and freeze until firm.

LEMON AND ELDERFLOWER SYLLABUB
Serves 2 – 3

300ml, ½pt double cream
2 tbsp elderflower cordial
1 tbsp lemon juice

Whip the cream and gently fold in the elderflower cordial and lemon juice. Serve chilled in glasses.

ELDERFLOWER & STRAWBERRY TRIFLE
Serves 6 - 8

For the base
225g, 8oz sponge cake
2 tbsp elderflower cordial + 2 tbsp marsala
225g, 8oz strawberries, sliced

Cream topping
flowers snipped from 1 elderflower head
juice and pared rind from 1 lemon
75g , 3oz icing sugar
300ml, ½pt double cream

Break up the sponge and cover the base of a round serving bowl. Sprinkle the cordial and marsala over the sponge. Arrange the sliced strawberries over the sponge. Put the lemon juice and rind in a small bowl and add the elderflowers. Allow to infuse for at least 30 minutes, then strain and beat the double cream and icing sugar into the juice. Spread over the strawberries and chill before serving.

STRAWBERRY AND ELDERFLOWER JAM
Makes about 2.7kg, 6lb

1.35kg, 3lb strawberries, hulled and chopped
1.35kg, 3lb granulated sugar
juice of 1 lemon
50g, 2oz redcurrants, puréed and sieved
2 handfuls of elderflowers, stripped from stalks

Put the strawberries, granulated sugar, lemon juice and
redcurrant purée in a preserving pan and add the
elderflowers. Cover the pan and leave in a warm place
for 2 or 3 hours. Place the pan over a gentle heat and
stir until the sugar dissolves. Raise the heat and boil
rapidly. After about 15 minutes test for a set. If it is not
ready, boil for a little longer and test again. Turn off
the heat and leave in the pan for 20 minutes before
pouring into warmed jars and sealing.

GOOSEBERRY AND ELDERFLOWER JAM
Makes 2.7kg, 6lb

2kg, 4.4lb gooseberries
16 elderflower heads
2 litres, 4pts water
2kg, 4.4lb granulated sugar

Put the gooseberries in a preserving pan with the water
and cook for about 30 minutes until the gooseberries
are soft. Add the granulated sugar and heat gently to
dissolve the sugar. Meanwhile remove the stalks from
the elderflowers and put in a muslin bag. Add to the
pan and bring the gooseberries to the boil and boil
rapidly until setting point is reached. Pour into warmed
jars and seal.

LEMON AND ELDERFLOWER CURD
Makes 675g, 1½lb

2 handfuls of elderflowers, stripped from their stems
100g, 4oz butter, cubed
225g, 8oz granulated sugar
3 eggs + 1 egg yolk
finely grated rind and juice of 3 lemons

Put the elderflowers in a large bowl with all the other ingredients and place over a pan of boiling water. Stir the mixture until it thickens and coats the back of the spoon. Pour into warmed jars and cover. This will keep in the fridge for a couple of weeks.

ELDERFLOWER JELLY
Makes about 1.35kg, 3lb

This jelly goes well with chicken, game, pork or lamb.

20 elderflower heads, stalks removed
1.35kg, 3lb cooking apples, chopped
3 tbsp white wine vinegar
granulated sugar

Put the apples, elderflowers and vinegar in a large saucepan with 900ml, 1½pt of water. Bring to the boil and simmer until soft. Strain through a muslin bag overnight. Measure the liquid and for every 600ml or 1pt of liquid add 450g or 1lb of sugar. Return to the saucepan and cook gently allowing the sugar to dissolve, then bring to a rapid boil. Boil until setting

point is reached – this may take up to 25 minutes. Pour
into warmed jars and seal.

ELDERBERRY AND APPLE CRUMBLE
Serves 6

225g, 8oz elderberries, washed and stalks removed
675g, 1½lb cooking apples, peeled, cored and sliced
2 tbsp water
100g, 4oz granulated sugar

Crumble

125g, 5oz wholemeal flour
100g, 4oz butter
75g, 3oz light muscovado sugar
50g, 2oz ground hazelnuts

Put the elderberries and apples in a baking dish with
the water and add the granulated sugar, turning the fruit
over as you do so, to distribute the sugar evenly. To
make the crumble whiz the flour, butter, sugar and
hazelnuts in a food processor until the mixture
resembles breadcrumbs and then spread over the fruit,
patting it down gently. Bake in the oven at gas mark 4,
180°C (350°F) for 30 minutes.

PEAR AND ELDERBERRY
UPSIDE DOWN PUDDING
Serves 4 – 6

knob of butter
25g, 1oz brown sugar
4 pears, peeled and sliced
175g, 6oz elderberries, stalks removed
175g, 6oz self-raising flour
175g, 6oz butter
175g, 6oz granulated sugar
3 eggs
2 tbsp milk

Rub the butter around the base of a 20cm, 8in round cake tin and sprinkle with the brown sugar. Arrange the sliced pears and elderberries in the tin. To make the sponge whiz all the rest of the ingredients up in the food processor. Spread evenly over the pears and bake in the oven for 45 minutes at gas mark 4, 180°C (350°F) or until a skewer inserted in the sponge comes out clean. Turn out so that the pears and elderberries are on top. Serve with Greek yoghurt or cream.

ELDERBERRY SORBET
Serves 4 – 6

450g, 1lb elderberries, stalks removed
175g, 6oz granulated sugar
300ml, ½pt water
juice of ½ a lemon
1 egg white

Whiz the elderberries up in the food processor and then sieve them to remove pips. Dissolve the granulated sugar in the water and boil for 5 minutes. Stir in the elderberry purée and the lemon juice. Freeze until the slushy stage then whisk up the mixture to break down ice crystals. Whisk the egg white until stiff and fold this in. Freeze again until firm.

ELDERBERRY AND BLACKBERRY JAM
Makes 1.35kg, 3lb

450g, 1lb elderberries, stalks removed
450g, 1lb blackberries
4 tbsp lemon juice
900g, 2lb granulated sugar

Put the elderberries and blackberries in a large saucepan. Heat them gently and allow to simmer until they release plenty of juice. Sieve the pulp to remove all the pips. Return to the pan , add the granulated sugar and lemon juice and boil until setting point is reached. Pour into warm jars and seal.

ELDERBERRY AND APPLE JELLY

Yield will vary depending on the juiciness of the fruit - 1kg or 2lb of sugar should yield 1.5kg or just over 3lb of jelly.

900g, 2lb elderberries, stalks removed
1.35kg, 3lb cooking apples, chopped
water
peel from 1 orange
5cm, 2in cinnamon stick
granulated sugar

Combine the apples, elderberries, orange peel and cinnamon stick with water to cover in a large saucepan. Simmer until the fruit is soft. Discard the orange peel and cinnamon stick. Strain through muslin overnight. Measure the liquid and for every 600ml or or 1pt of liquid add 450g or 1lb of sugar. Dissolve the granulated sugar over a gentle heat and then bring to a rapid boil. Boil until setting point is reached – this may take up to 25 minutes. Pour into warmed jars and seal.

ELDERBERRY CHUTNEY

675g, 1½lb elderberries, stalks removed
450g, 1lb onions, peeled and diced
675g, 1½lb cooking apples, peeled, cored & chopped
1 tsp mixed spice
1 tsp ground ginger
½ tsp cayenne pepper
½ tsp salt
450ml, ¾pt vinegar
350g, 12oz granulated sugar

Put the elderberries, onions and apples in a large saucepan. Add the spices, salt and half the vinegar. Bring to the boil, then turn down and simmer for 30 minutes. Add the granulated sugar and the remaining vinegar. Stir until the sugar has dissolved and then simmer until thick, stirring to prevent sticking. This should take about 40 minutes. Spoon into warmed jars and seal. Try to keep for 6 weeks to mature.

ELDERBERRY AND APPLE SAUCE

A piquant sauce to serve with meat.

2 large cooking apples, peeled, cored and sliced
100g, 4oz elderberries, stalks removed
3 tbsp water
1 tbsp granulated sugar

Put the apples and elderberries in a saucepan and add the water and granulated sugar. Simmer until the apples are soft. Serve warm or cold.

FIGS

Figs were said to have grown in the Garden of Eden with their leaves covering the nakedness of Adam and Eve. Figs probably originated in Asia Minor and were one of the first fruits to have been cultivated. They were known to the Egyptians at the time of the Pharaohs and were a favoured fruit of the Greeks and Romans. In 400BC Aristophanes wrote 'Nothing is sweeter than figs'. The Romans introduced them to Britain, planting fig trees wherever they conquered land.

The fig is a member of the mulberry family. Figs are produced singly or in pairs in the leaf axils and are classified by the colour of their skins – there are white, purple, black and red varieties. Trees in England grow best in the South often up against a south facing wall. It is advisable to confine the root growth as this encourages fruiting. Outdoor figs try to produce two crops a year but in our climate only one crop ripens. The first crop is usually ready for picking when the fruit is soft and the skin is about to split – this is usually in August or early September. The tree will also produce tiny new figs in the autumn – these should be left and will mature the following summer. There will also be slightly larger figs that will not have time to mature before the frosts – these are the ones you should pick and discard to allow the tree to concentrate its energies on the smaller ones.

Fresh figs do not travel well so there is a thriving market is for dried figs. Smyrna figs are imported dried from Turkey. California is also an important growing area and it is one of the biggest exporters of dried figs.

Fresh figs contain around 80% water and 12% sugar however when they are dried the sugar increases to 50% - this is why dried figs are useful in cakes and puddings. Fresh figs can be eaten with their skin on. Figs are well known for their laxative properties. They are a good source of calcium, are rich in iron and are high in fibre.

Drying Figs - you can dry your own figs if you have a good supply. In hot countries this is done by spreading the fruit out in the sun and turning them to expose each side. In this country you may have to dry your figs on a hot, sunny windowsill.

FIGS WITH HONEY AND WINE
Serves 3 – 4

450g, 1lb fresh green figs
150ml, ¼pt dry white wine
3 tbsp honey

Wash the figs, and trim the stems. Put in a saucepan and add the wine. Bring slowly to the boil and add the honey. Cover and simmer for 15 minutes. Remove the figs with a slotted spoon and transfer to a serving dish. Boil the syrup for 10 minutes to reduce and thicken it. Pour it over the fruit. Chill before serving.

FIGS WITH HAM AND GINGER DRESSING
Serves 8 as a starter

8 fresh figs
8 slices of Parma ham
25g, 1oz stem ginger
2 tbsp syrup from the stem ginger jar
3 tbsp olive oil
1 tsp lemon juice
sprinkling of black pepper

Halve the figs and arrange on a serving dish with the Parma ham draped over the figs. For the dressing, chop the stem ginger and add the syrup, oil, lemon juice and pepper. Whisk together and pour over the figs and ham.

APPLE AND FIG CRUMBLE
Serves 4 - 6

Filling
100g, 4oz figs, halved
150ml, ¼pt water
675g, 1½lb cooking apples, peeled, cored and chopped
75g, 3oz granulated sugar

Crumble
50g, 2oz plain flour
50g, 2oz porridge oats
50g, 2oz ground almonds
75g, 3oz margarine
50g, 2oz brown sugar

Put the figs in a saucepan with the water and simmer for 5 minutes. Mix with the apples and granulated sugar in a baking dish and pour over the remaining liquid. Put the flour and oats in a bowl with the ground almonds. Add the margarine and rub with the fingertips until the mixture resembles breadcrumbs. Stir in the brown sugar. Spread this crumble mixture over the apples and figs and cook at gas mark 4, 180°C (350°F) for 30 minutes.

FIG SORBET
Serves 4

8 ripe figs
300ml, ½pt water
100g, 4oz caster sugar
1 tbsp lemon juice
1 egg white

Process the figs. Don't worry about the skin – you can leave this on. Rub the purée through a sieve to remove the pips. Make a sugar syrup by heating the water and caster sugar gently until the sugar has dissolved. Then boil for 5 minutes. Add the lemon juice and the fig purée. Put into the freezer and freeze until the slushy stage. Then whisk the mixture to break down ice crystals. Whisk the egg white until stiff and fold this into the fig mixture. Return to the freezer and freeze until firm.

FIG, DATE AND WALNUT LOAF
Serves 8

100g, 4oz dried figs, chopped
100g, 4oz dates, chopped
150ml, ¼pt boiling water
75g, 3oz butter
75g, 3oz dark brown sugar
1 egg
225g, 8oz self-raising flour
1 tsp baking powder
75g, 3oz walnuts, chopped

Put the figs and dates in a bowl and pour the boiling water over them. Leave for a few minutes to soften. Combine the butter, sugar, egg, flour and baking powder. Beat until everything is mixed together. Stir in the figs and dates with the water and the walnuts. Spoon the mixture into a 1kg, 2lb greased loaf tin and bake in the oven at gas mark 4, 180°C (350°F) for 1 hour or until a skewer inserted into the loaf comes out clean.

FIG AND GINGER SHORTBREAD
Makes 8 slices

175g, 6oz plain flour
1 tsp ground ginger
100g, 4oz butter
85g, 3½oz light brown sugar
40g, 1½oz dried figs, chopped

You can either whiz all the ingredients up in a food processor, adding the chopped figs as soon as the mixture starts to bind together or cream together the butter and sugar and then gradually work in the flour sifted with the ginger. Lastly mix in the figs. Press into a 23cm, 9in flan tin and prick all over with a fork. Bake in the oven at gas mark 4, 180°C (350°F) for 25 minutes or until browned on top.

FIG AND DATE SHORTCAKE BARS
Makes 15 slices

For the filling

100g, 4oz dried figs
100g, 4oz dates
2 tbsp water
1 tbsp honey
1 tbsp lemon juice

For the shortbread

175g, 6oz flour
50g, 2oz semolina
100g, 4oz butter
100g, 4oz caster sugar

To make the filling put the figs and dates in a saucepan with the water, honey and lemon juice. Bring the mixture to the boil, then lower the heat and simmer for 10 minutes. Put into a food processor and purée. To make the shortbread combine all the ingredients in a processor and process until the mixture binds together. Press just over half the mixture into the base of a 20cm, 8in greased square tin. Smooth the base and spread the fig and date mixture on top. Roll out the remaining shortbread mixture to fit over the filling and press down to cover. Bake in the oven at gas mark 4, 180°C (350°F) for 25 minutes and cut into slices while still warm.

FIG AND LEMON JAM
Makes 2.5kg, 5lb

900g, 2lb fresh figs, washed, stalks removed
1.2 litres, 2pts cold water
1.35kg, 3lb granulated sugar
grated rind and juice of 4 lemons

Put the figs in the water in a large bowl and leave to soak for 24 hours. Transfer to a large saucepan and add the sugar. Cook gently to dissolve the sugar and then bring to the boil. Remove any scum. Add the lemon rind and juice to the figs and boil until setting point is reached. Pour into warmed jars and seal.

HAWTHORN BERRIES

Hawthorns are prolific all over Britain showing up on the edges of fields, in hedges, woodland edges, scrubland and on roadside verges. The hawthorn is a deciduous shrub or small tree, also called the May tree. The tree features in folklore and was said to have healing powers and also to offer protection against lightning. The hawthorn is meant to be a symbol of re-birth and life. Some say that Christ wore a crown of hawthorn.

You can pick the young leaves in April and use them in salads. These young leaves used to be known to children as 'bread and cheese'. The hawthorn produces an abundance of strongly scented white or pink blossom in May. The leaves are deeply lobed on spiny branches. In the autumn hawthorn berries or haws can be picked and used in jellies. Haws are the most abundant berries in the autumn, each bush producing bunches of round, dark red berries, lasting well into January. They are fiddly to pick and destalk and are a dry fruit, with a large pip, so need quite a lot of water (which they absorb) when cooking the fruit for a jelly.

The azarole is a relation of the hawthorn and produces larger yellow, orange or red fruits. These are grown commercially and the fruit used for flavouring liqueurs.

HAW JELLY

Yield will vary depending on the juiciness of the fruit - 1kg or 2lb of sugar should yield 1.5kg or just over 3lb of jelly. Haws makes a beautiful red jelly.

1kg, 2.2lb haws
1.2 litres, 2pts water
juice of 1 lemon
granulated sugar

Wash and get rid of as many of the stalks on the haws as possible. Put in a large pan with the water and simmer for 1 hour. The berries will absorb a lot of water. Pour into a muslin bag and allow to strain overnight. Do not squeeze the bag, as you will then not get a clear jelly. Measure the juice and allow 450g or 1lb of sugar for each 600ml or 1pt of juice. Return the haw juice to the pan and add the granulated sugar. Add the lemon juice and heat gently until the sugar dissolves, then boil rapidly until the jelly will set. Pour into warmed jars and seal.

HAW, APPLE AND ELDERBERRY JELLY

Yield will vary depending on the juiciness of the fruit
- 1kg or 2lb of sugar should yield 1.5kg or just over
3lb of jelly.

450g, 1lb haws, stalks removed
450g, 1lb crab apples
450g, 1lb elderberries, stalks removed
water
granulated sugar

Combine all the fruits in a large saucepan and cover
with water. Bring to the boil and simmer until softened,
crushing the fruits on the sides of the saucepan to extract
the juices. Pour into a muslin bag and allow to strain
overnight. Measure the juice and allow 450g or 1lb of
sugar for each 600ml or 1pt of juice. Return the fruit
juice to the pan and add the lemon juice and sugar.
Heat gently until the sugar dissolves, then boil rapidly
until the jelly will set. Pour into warmed jars and seal.

HAW SAUCE

675g, 1½lb haws
450ml, ¾pt white wine vinegar
100g, 4oz granulated sugar
25g, 1oz salt

Put the haws in a large pan with the vinegar and simmer
for 30 minutes. Then sieve the haws and return to the
pan with the sugar and salt. Boil for 10 minutes. Pour
into small bottles and seal.

MEDLARS

Medlar trees originated in Persia. The Greeks and Romans were both familiar with them – Theophrastus mentioned medlars and later Pliny referred to three different types. The name, 'medlar' derives from the Greek for 'mesos' meaning half and 'pilos' meaning ball. They were once popular in Britain, reaching their peak during the Middle Ages in Europe. Charlemagne decreed that the medlar be planted on the royal estates and medlars were common in monastery gardens. In Victorian times they were reasonably popular and used to be served at the end of a meal with port. Today medlar trees are a rare sight and the fruit is not widely used or known about. If you are lucky, you might know someone with a medlar tree in his or her garden – the fruit is prolific and you don't need much to make a medlar jelly or cheese (see recipes below).

Occasionally you might find one in hedgerows in the south of England. You are unlikely to find them on sale anywhere. Medlar trees are similar to pear trees, being fairly low with branches and trunk often contorted. The leaves are lance-shaped and the tree produces white, scentless flowers in May. The fruit is greenish-yellow when unripe, looking like a small apple and later on looks like a giant brown rose hip with its five-tailed calyx sticking out from the head of the fruit like a crown. The French have a rather rude term for the medlar – 'cul de chien' which we loosely translate as 'dog's arse'.

Medlar fruits have to be half rotten or 'bletted' before they are edible. Fruits do not have time to fully ripen on the tree in Britain as in Mediterranean countries.

They must be picked in late autumn or left to fall and stored until they become soft and look like a rotten pear. The foliage turns a beautiful reddish brown in the autumn. The fruit, once bletted, can be eat with a little cream and sugar but first you have to extract the flesh from the five large pips and remove the skin which can prove tedious. The taste is difficult to describe – it's a bit like apple purée with a hint of cinnamon. Some say they taste like dates but less sweet. The easiest solution is to make jelly which keeps and can be used for sweet or savoury purposes. Nutritionally medlars are high in potassium.

MEDLAR JELLY
Makes about 1.1kg, 2½lb

Using some unripe medlars increases the pectin and makes a well flavoured jelly.

1.8kg, 4lb medlars, bletted
or half bletted and half unripe
water to cover
juice of 1 lemon
granulated sugar

Wash the medlars and put into a large saucepan with water to cover. Add the lemon juice and bring to the boil. Simmer for about 1 hour by which time the fruit will be very soft. Strain the fruit through muslin without squeezing. Measure the liquid and for every 600ml or 1pt of juice use 450g or 1lb of sugar. Heat the juice gently with the sugar in a large preserving pan until the sugar has dissolved. Bring to the boil and

test for a set after about 15 minutes. When ready pour into warmed jars and seal.

MEDLAR AND APPLE JELLY

Yield will vary depending on the juiciness of the fruit - 1kg or 2lb of sugar should yield 1.5kg or just over 3lb of jelly.

1.35kg, 3lb medlars
1.35kg, 3lb russet apples, unpeeled, cut into chunks
2 lemons
6 cloves
granulated sugar

Wash the medlars and put into a large saucepan with the apples. Squeeze the juice from the lemons and add to the pan. Stick the cloves into some of the lemon rind and add them as well. Just cover the fruit with water and bring to the boil. Simmer for about 1 hour by which time the fruit will be very soft. Strain the fruit through muslin and allow the juice to drain through without squeezing. Measure the liquid and for every 600ml or 1pt of juice use 450g or 1lb of sugar. Heat the juice gently with the sugar in a large preserving pan until the sugar has dissolved. Bring to the boil and skim off any scum from the surface. Test for a set after about 20 minutes. When ready pour into warmed jars and seal.

MEDLAR CHEESE

1kg, 2.2lb medlars
granulated sugar

Use bletted medlars and sieve them so that you have a smooth purée. Discard the skins and pips. Add an equal amount of sugar to the medlar purée and heat gently. Simmer the mixture, stirring every so often to prevent any sticking to the bottom of the saucepan and continue to cook until the cheese is very thick. Spoon into oiled moulds and store. This is good with cheese or cold meats.

MEDLAR PURÉE WITH CREAM AND SUGAR

450g, 1lb medlars
75g, 3oz brown sugar
150ml, ¼pt thick cream
½ tsp cinnamon

Sieve the medlars and mix the purée with brown sugar, cream and cinnamon.

MULBERRIES

Black mulberries are native to Western Asia. The Greeks and Romans grew them – Pliny the Elder called them the wisest of trees. The Roman emperor, Justinian encouraged the planting of mulberry trees for the silk worms to feed on. The Romans brought them to Britain and they were popular in the Middle Ages. James I encouraged people to grow them and introduced large numbers to London to promote the silk industry.

There are two types of mulberry: the Black and the White. The White Mulberry produces inferior fruit but is a more decorative tree and the silk worms prefer it. Mulberries grow on medium sized trees which are slow to grow but live to a grand old age and often look gnarled. There are records showing that some mulberry trees have survived 600 years. The Black mulberry produces the best fruit – rather like very dark loganberries with a pleasant but slightly acidic taste. The berries drop to the ground as they ripen in late August. Beware though because they stain all that they touch. Then as soon as autumn arrives the trees shed their leaves. New trees will bear fruit after about five years. You can buy mulberry trees as two or three year olds and they will look fantastic in the centre of your lawn. The type to go for is Chelsea, because it is noted for its early cropping. Mulberries are versatile and can be used for jams and jellies as well as in puddings on their own or combined with other fruits. Mulberries are very high in potassium and are a good source of calcium, phosphorus and vitamin C.

MULBERRY MUFFINS
Makes 12

225g, 8oz plain flour
2 tsp baking powder
50g, 2oz caster sugar
300ml, ½pt milk
1 egg, beaten
50g, 2oz butter
100g, 4oz mulberries

Sift the flour and baking powder and add the caster sugar. Make a well in the centre and add the milk and egg. Mix together and then gradually beat in the butter. Fold in the mulberries. Divide the mixture between 12 greased muffin cases. Bake in the oven at gas mark 6, 200°C (400°F) for 20 minutes.

MULBERRY CLAFOUTIS
Serves 4 – 6

50g, 2oz flour
50g, 2oz + 1 tbsp caster sugar
1 tbsp sunflower oil
2 eggs + 1 egg yolk
300ml, ½pt milk
450g, 1lb mulberries
25g, 1oz butter, diced

Stir the flour and caster sugar together. Beat in the oil, eggs and milk. Arrange the mulberries in a greased baking dish. Pour the batter over them and dot with the butter. Bake in the oven at gas mark 4, 180°C (350°F) for about 30 minutes until the batter is risen and browned. Sprinkle the tablespoon of caster sugar over the batter and serve with cream.

MULBERRY AND PEAR
UPSIDE DOWN PUDDING
Serves 4 – 6

100g, 4oz golden syrup
100g, 4oz mulberries
3 pears, peeled, cored and sliced
grated rind of 1 lemon

For the cake

100g, 4oz butter
100g, 4oz brown sugar
100g, 4oz self-raising flour
2 eggs
2 tbsp milk

Spoon the golden syrup into the base of a lightly greased 20cm, 8in deep round cake tin. Arrange the mulberries and pear slices over the golden syrup and scatter the lemon rind on as well. To make the sponge beat together all the ingredients and spoon over the fruit. Bake in the oven at gas mark 4, 180°C (350°F) for 35 minutes and cool in the tin a little before turning out. Serve warm with cream.

MULBERRY AND PEACH
SUMMER PUDDING
Serves 4

675g, 1½lb mulberries
225g, 8oz peaches, de-stoned and diced
2 tbsp water
175g, 6oz caster sugar
8 slices brown bread, crusts removed

Put the mulberries and diced peaches with the water
and sugar in a saucepan and heat gently until the juices
run. Simmer until the fruit is soft. Use the bread to
line a 900ml, 2pt pudding basin. Pour the fruit over
the bread and top with remaining bread. Place a saucer
and weight on top of the bread – this helps the juices
to colour the bread. Leave in the fridge overnight. When
ready, turn the pudding out and serve with crème fraîche
or Greek yoghurt.

MULBERRY AND APPLE ICE CREAM
Serves 4 – 6

450g, 1lb mulberries
225g, 8oz cooking apples, peeled, cored and sliced
3 eggs, separated
175g, 6oz caster sugar
300ml, ½pt double cream, whipped

Heat the mulberries and apples gently in a saucepan
and cook until they become juicy and soften. Purée
and sieve them. Whisk the egg yolks with the sugar

until thick and fold into the fruit purée. Add the cream and stir until well incorporated. Lastly whisk the egg whites until stiff and fold them in. Make sure everything is well combined and transfer to a freezer container. Freeze until firm and remove from the freezer about 10 minutes before serving.

MULBERRY YOGHURT ICE
Serves 4

450g, 1lb mulberries
150ml, ¼pt plain yoghurt
100g, 4oz icing sugar
2 tbsp lemon juice
150ml, ¼pt double cream, whipped
2 egg whites

Heat the mulberries gently in a saucepan and cook until they become juicy and soften. Purée and sieve them. Mix the mulberry purée, yoghurt, icing sugar and lemon juice together until smooth. Fold the whipped cream into the mulberry mixture. Pour into a container and freeze until just becoming firm. Whisk the egg whites until stiff and fold them into the half frozen ice cream. Return to the freezer and freeze until firm.

MULBERRY JAM
Makes about 2.7kg, 6lb

2kg, 4½lb mulberries, under-ripe and unwashed
2kg, 4½lb granulated sugar

Put the mulberries in a large saucepan, and gently heat them until the juices start to run. Leave to cook slowly for 30 minutes. Meanwhile warm the granulated sugar and add to the mulberries. Cook for another 15 minutes, or until all the sugar has dissolved. Then boil the jam on the highest heat for 10 minutes. Spoon a little onto a plate and push with your finger to see if it crinkles. If not boil for a few more minutes and test again until the jam has set. Leave for 15 minutes, adding a little knob of butter to get rid of any scum. Pour into warmed jars and seal.

MULBERRY AND APPLE JELLY

Yield will vary depending on the juiciness of the fruit - 1kg or 2lb of sugar should yield 1.5kg or just over 3lb of jelly.

450g, 1lb cooking apples
300ml, ½pt water
1kg, 2.2lb mulberries
granulated sugar

Cut the apples up but do not peel or core them. Put in a large saucepan with the water and cook for 10 minutes. Then add the mulberries and cook until soft. Strain through a muslin bag overnight. Measure the

liquid and for every 600ml or 1pt of liquid add 450g or 1lb of sugar. Over the heat allow the sugar to dissolve and then bring to a rapid boil. Boil until setting point is reached – this may take up to 25 minutes. Pour into warmed, sterilised jars and seal.

MULBERRY SYRUP

1kg, 2.2lb mulberries
granulated sugar

Put the mulberries in a larger saucepan and cook gently with a little water until the juices run and the mulberries are soft. Sieve the mulberries and to every 600ml or 1pt of juice add 450g or 1lb of sugar. Heat gently until the sugar dissolves. Pour the syrup into a couple of bottles and put the bottles in a deep pan on a folded tea cloth. Add water to come up to the necks of the bottles. Heat the water to simmering point and simmer for 20 minutes. This will sterilise the bottles. Remove and cool before sealing well.

QUINCES

Originally from Persia and Turkestan, quinces were popular with the Greeks and Romans. The quince features as the golden apple in Greek myths and was dedicated to Aphrodite, as the symbol of love and happiness. The golden apples of Hesperides were thought to have been quinces. The Greeks believed that the trees sprung up wherever Aphrodite stepped when she came out of the foaming sea. In the Jewish religion it is believed that the serpent tempted Eve with a quince rather than an apple. Quinces were being grown in Britain during the time of Edward I - records show that he planted four trees at The Tower of London. In the early 1600s John Tradescant brought the 'Portugal' quince to Britain and the fruits were popular from then on until going into decline in the 1900s. However they are now making a comeback and the Brogdale Horticultural Trust have a 4 acre commercial quince orchard featuring 19 different varieties. A wild version of the quince can still be found in Iran.

The quince tree makes an attractive tree in the garden with beautiful pale pink blossom in May. It is a small, spreading deciduous tree which is long lived and develops knotted, interesting-looking branches. The quince is a member of the rose family and bears a golden yellow fruit shaped rather like a fat pear. The trees appear to be self-fertile since single trees in gardens bear good crops of fruit. As the fruit ripens it changes from green to yellow. The flesh is hard and granular and cannot be eaten raw. The fruit has a strong and pleasant aroma and should be stored separately from other fruit. When cooked the flesh turns pink and soft. Quinces make great jelly and a wonderful fruit cheese of which the Spanish version is called

membrillo. They combine well with apples and pears in fruit puddings. Quinces are eaten in the Middle East with meat, such as lamb. Indeed in Persian cookery quinces have featured for at least the last 2,000 years in sweet and savoury dishes.

The quince contains a great deal of pectin especially when it is slightly unripe, so can be combined with other fruits to make jams. Quinces are high in potassium and vitamin A. They are rich in soluble fibre and are known to calm the stomach and allay nausea.

ROASTED PORK WITH QUINCES
Serves 6 - 8

4 quinces, peeled, quartered and cored
300ml, ½pt apple juice
peel from ½ a lemon
2 tbsp olive oil
1 tbsp Dijon mustard
1 tbsp fresh rosemary, chopped
1 small onion, peeled and finely chopped
loin of pork, approx 1.35kg, 3lb

Put the quinces in a saucepan with the apple juice and lemon peel, bring to the boil and then reduce the heat and simmer until the quinces are tender. Increase the heat and boil for 5 minutes to reduce the liquid. In a small bowl mix together the oil, mustard, rosemary and onion. Put the pork in a roasting tin and spread this mustard mixture over it. Roast in the oven at gas mark 5, 190°C (375°F) for 40 minutes and then pour the quince syrup over the pork and arrange the quince quarters round the joint. Roast for another 40 minutes. Serve the pork with the quinces and juices from the tin.

EASY QUINCE MOUSSE
Serves 4

450g, 1lb quinces, peeled, cored and chopped
2 tbsp water
2 eggs, separated
75g, 3oz caster sugar

Cook the quinces with the water, adding a little more if they become too dry. When soft, purée and sieve them. Beat the egg yolks with the sugar until thick. Stir into the quince purée. Beat the egg whites until stiff and fold these into the quince mixture. Transfer to a serving bowl and chill in the fridge. Serve, if liked, with crème fraiche and a drizzle of maple syrup.

QUINCE AND GINGER MOUSSE
Serves 4

2 pieces of stem ginger, finely chopped and 1 tbsp
syrup from the jar
300ml, ½pt quince purée (see previous recipe)
150ml, ¼pt double cream, whipped
2 egg whites

Stir the stem ginger and syrup into the quince purée. Fold in the double cream. Whisk the egg whites until stiff and fold them in as well. Spoon into a serving bowl and chill before serving.

QUINCE AND POLENTA
UPSIDE DOWN CAKE
Serves 6

175g, 6oz caster sugar
4 quinces, peeled, cored and sliced
juice of ½ a lemon
2 tbsp honey
100g, 4oz butter
3 eggs
1 tsp vanilla essence
100g, 4oz self-raising flour
50g, 2oz instant polenta

Caramel Sauce
225g, 8oz light muscovado sugar
2 tbsp milk
15g, ½oz butter

Grease a 20cm, 8in round cake tin and sprinkle two tablespoons of the caster sugar over the base. Arrange the quince slices over the sugar and sprinkle with lemon juice. Drizzle with the honey. To make the sponge, cream the butter with the rest of the caster sugar, beat in the eggs, vanilla essence and flour with the polenta. Spoon over the quinces and spread evenly. Bake in the oven at gas mark 4, 180°C (350°F) for about 40 minutes or until a skewer inserted in the sponge comes out clean. Turn out on to a serving plate. To make the sauce, heat the sugar, milk and butter together and boil all the ingredients together for exactly 7 minutes. Serve the cake with the sauce.

QUINCE AND GINGER CRUMBLE
Serves 6

450g, 1lb quinces, peeled, cored and chopped
450g, 1lb cooking apples, peeled, cored and sliced
2 tbsp water
100g, 4oz granulated sugar

For the crumble
175g, 6oz plain flour
2 tsp ground ginger
75g, 3oz butter
50g, 2oz brown sugar

Cook the apples and quinces with the water and granulated sugar for 5 – 10 minutes to soften them. Transfer to a baking dish. To make the crumble combine all the ingredients in a food processor and process until the mixture resembles breadcrumbs. Spread evenly over the fruit and bake in the oven at gas mark 4, 180°C (350°F) for about 30 minutes.

QUINCE MUFFINS
Makes 12

225g, 8oz plain flour
3 tsp baking powder
50g, 2oz caster sugar
2 eggs, beaten
150ml, ¼pt milk
50g, 2oz butter, melted
12 cubes of quince cheese (see page 80)

Sift the flour, baking powder and sugar into a bowl. Beat the eggs with the milk and mix in the butter. Stir this liquid into the flour. Spoon a little of the mixture into each greased muffin tin, add a cube of quince cheese and cover with more mixture so that each one is about half full. Bake in the oven at gas mark 6, 200°C (400°F) for 15 minutes.

SPICED QUINCES
Should make 2kg, 4½lb

1.35kg, 3lb quinces, peeled and cored
water
granulated sugar
white wine vinegar
coriander seeds

Cut the quinces into largish pieces, transfer to a saucepan and cover with water. Bring to the boil and simmer for 10 minutes. Strain and reserve the quinces. Measure the liquid and for every 600ml or 1pt of water add 450g, 1lb of sugar, 150ml, ¼pt of white wine vinegar and one teaspoon of coriander seeds. Put into a saucepan bring to the boil and stir until the sugar has dissolved. Replace the quinces and cook gently for about 30 minutes. Remove the fruit with a slotted spoon and pack into warm, sterilised jars. Bring the syrup back to the boil and boil for another two or three minutes, then pour over the quinces. Seal and store in a cool, dark place.

QUINCE PASTE/CHEESE

This is called pasta de membrillo in Spain. You can cut the paste into small squares and roll them in icing sugar if liked. Alternatively serve with cheese.

900g, 2lb peeled and cored quinces
300ml, ½pt water
granulated sugar

Cut the quinces into small pieces and put them in a large saucepan with the water. Bring to the boil and then simmer for 30 minutes until the fruit is soft. Pass through a sieve and measure the purée. For every 600ml or 1pt add 450g or 1lb of sugar and cook slowly stirring frequently until the purée thickens and forms a thick paste. Pour onto a greaseproof paper on a baking tray and leave to dry and set. Cut into squares and store in airtight containers. This paste keeps for ages.

APPLE AND QUINCE JELLY
Makes 1.5kg, 3¼lb

This goes well with meat such as lamb and pork or can be eaten with toast and butter. If the quinces are unripe the pectin content will be higher and the lemon juice is not quite so necessary. The apples also contain good quantities of pectin. This jelly is good spread on scones or as a filling for cakes but also can be served as an accompaniment for savoury dishes.

1kg, 2.2lb quinces, chopped
1.35kg, 3lb apples, chopped

granulated sugar
juice of 1 lemon

Combine the quinces and apples in a large saucepan with just enough water to cover them. Cook until the fruit is soft. Strain through a muslin bag overnight. Measure the liquid and for every 600ml or 1pt of liquid add 450g or 1lb of sugar. Add the lemon juice and over the heat allow the sugar to dissolve and then bring to a rapid boil. Boil until setting point is reached – this may take up to 25 minutes. Pour into warmed, sterilised jars and seal.

QUINCE CONSERVE

This is similar to jam but the fruit is conserved in pieces.

6 large quinces, peeled and cored
450g, 1lb granulated sugar
900ml, 1½pts water
2 tbsp lemon juice
5cm, 2in cinnamon stick
2 whole cloves
2 tbsp rosewater

Cut the quinces into pieces. In a large saucepan dissolve the granulated sugar in the water and bring to the boil. Add the quince pieces, lemon juice, cinnamon stick, cloves and rosewater and boil for 3 or 4 minutes. Lower the heat and simmer for about 2 minutes, stirring until the syrup thickens and coats the back of a spoon. Turn off the heat, take out the cinnamon stick and cloves and when cooled pour into warmed jars and seal.

QUINCE AND BLACKBERRY JELLY

Yield will vary depending on the juiciness of the fruit
- 1kg or 2lb of sugar should yield 1.5kg or just over
3lb of jelly.

1kg, 2.2lb quinces, chopped
1kg, 2.2lb blackberries
water
granulated sugar

Put the chopped quinces, including skin and cores in a
large saucepan with enough water to cover. Bring to
the boil and simmer for 15 minutes. Add the
blackberries and simmer for another 15 minutes. Strain
the fruit overnight through muslin. Measure the liquid
and for every 600ml or 1pt of liquid add 450g or 1lb of
sugar. Over the heat allow the sugar to dissolve and
then bring to a rapid boil. Boil until setting point is
reached – this may take up to 25 minutes. Pour into
warmed, sterilised jars and seal.

QUINCE VODKA

900g, 2lb whole quinces, grated
225g, 8oz granulated sugar
vodka

Grate the quinces and place in a 1 litre or 2 pint jar.
Add the sugar and fill up with vodka. Leave for at least
two months, then strain and bottle.

ROSEHIPS

Rosehips are found everywhere in hedgerows and on roadside verges. They are fiddly and time consuming to pick as the stems are thorny. They are also difficult to use in cooking because of their tiny hairy pips which have to be extracted. They are best used to make syrup or jams and jellies with apples. Rosehips are very high in vitamin C and were collected on a huge scale during the Second World War to make syrup.

ROSEHIP SYRUP
Makes about 1.5 litres, 2½pts

1kg, 2.2lb rosehips
2½ litres, 4½pts water
450g, 1lb granulated sugar

Wash the rosehips and remove all the stalks. Process briefly in a food processor. Put them into a saucepan with half the water, bring to the boil and boil for 20 minutes. Strain through a muslin bag, leaving the juice to drip through for at least 2 hours. Then take the rosehips and boil with the remaining water for 15 minutes. Strain the liquid again. You should have about 1 litre, 1¾ pints – add the sugar and stir over a low heat until the sugar has dissolved. Increase the heat and boil for 10 minutes. Pour into warmed sterilised bottles and seal. Stand the bottles on a folded cloth in a deep pan, filling it with water up to the necks of the bottles. Bring to the boil and boil for 10 minutes. This should help preserve the syrup. Store in a cool dark place. Once opened the bottles of syrup will not keep for more than a few days.

APPLE AND ROSEHIP JAM
Makes about 1.35kg, 3lb

1kg, 2.2lb rosehips
1.2 litres, 2pts water
1kg, 2.2lb apples, peeled, cored and chopped
900g, 2lb granulated sugar
2 tbsp lemon juice

Boil the rosehips in the water, crushing them against the sides of the pan until soft. Strain through muslin overnight. Cook the apples in a small amount of water (just enough to stop them burning) until soft. Add the rosehip juice, the granulated sugar and the lemon juice and heat gently until the sugar has dissolved. Then boil for about 15 – 20 minutes until setting point is reached. Transfer to warmed, sterilised jars and seal.

APPLE AND ROSEHIP JELLY

Yield will vary depending on the juiciness of the fruit - 1kg or 2lb of sugar should yield 1.5kg or just over 3lb of jelly.

1.35kg, 3lb cooking apples
675g, 1½lb rosehips
granulated sugar

Chop up the apples without peeling or coring them and put into a large preserving pan with the rosehips. Just cover with water and bring to the boil. Simmer,

crushing the rosehips against the sides of the pan to release the flesh until the apples are soft. Strain the fruit through a muslin bag overnight. Measure the liquid and for every 600ml or 1 pt of liquid add 450g or 1lb of sugar. Over the heat allow the sugar to dissolve and then bring to a rapid boil. Boil until setting point is reached – this may take up to 25 minutes. Pour into warmed, sterilised jars and seal.

APPLE AND ROSEHIP CHEESE

900g, 2lb cooking apples
175g, 6oz rosehips
300ml, ½pt orange juice
150ml, ¼pt water
granulated sugar

Wash and chop the unpeeled and uncored apples. Chop up the rosehips in a food processor and place them in a muslin bag. Put the apples and muslin bag (tied to secure the rosehips) in a preserving pan with the orange juice and water. Cook over a gentle heat until the apples are soft. Discard the muslin bag. Sieve the rosehip flavoured apples and weigh the purée. For every 450g, 1lb of apple purée allow 350g, 12oz of sugar. Return to the saucepan and simmer for at least 1 hour until very thick. Stir frequently to prevent the mixture sticking to the bottom of the pan. Spoon into jars or oiled moulds and seal.

ROSEHIP, HAW AND SLOE JELLY

Yield will vary depending on the juiciness of the fruit - 1kg or 2lb of sugar should yield 1.5kg or just over 3lb of jelly.

225g, 8oz rosehips, stalks removed
100g, 4oz haws, stalks removed
225g, 8oz sloes
450g, 1lb cooking apples, chopped
water
granulated sugar

Combine all the fruits in a large preserving pan and cover with water. Cook until the fruits are soft, crushing the rosehips, haws and sloes against the side of the pan. Strain the fruit through a muslin bag overnight. Measure the liquid and for every 600ml or 1pt of liquid add a 450g or 1lb of sugar. Over the heat allow the sugar to dissolve and then bring to a rapid boil. Boil until setting point is reached – this may take up to 25 minutes. Pour into warmed, sterilised jars and seal.

APPLE AND ROSEHIP
SHORTCAKE CRUMBLE
Serves 4

675g, 1½lb cooking apples, peeled, cored and sliced
3 tbsp rosehip syrup
175g, 6oz plain flour
75g, 3oz caster sugar
50g, 2oz butter

Layer the apple slices in a baking dish and pour the syrup over them. Process the flour, caster sugar and butter in a food processor until crumbly. Spread over the apples, patting down to cover the apple completely. Bake in the oven at gas mark 4, 180°C (350°F) for 30 minutes and serve hot with cream.

ROSEHIP AND APPLE MERINGUE
Serves 3 – 4

2 tbsp rosehip syrup
450g, 1lb apple purée
2 egg whites
100g, 4oz caster sugar

Add the rosehip syrup to the apple purée and spoon into an ovenproof dish. Whisk the egg whites until stiff and gradually whisk in the caster sugar. Spoon over the purée and bake in the oven at gas mark 4, 180°C (350°F) for 20 minutes or until the meringue topping is browned and crisp. The meringue underneath will be like marshmallow.

ROSEHIP AND APPLE SNOW
Serves 6

450g, 1lb cooking apples, peeled, cored and sliced
2 tbsp water
1 tbsp lemon juice
2 tbsp clear honey
150ml, ¼pt rosehip syrup
2 tbsp gelatine + 4 tbsp hot water
2 egg whites

Cook the apples with the water, lemon juice and honey until soft. Stir in the rosehip syrup. Stir the gelatine into the hot water and blend into the apple and rosehip. Whisk the egg whites until stiff and fold them into the mixture. Transfer into a glass bowl and put in the fridge to set.

ROSEHIP SYRUP ICE CREAM
Serves 4 – 6

2 tbsp rosehip syrup
300ml, ½pt apple purée
3 eggs, separated
75g, 3oz caster sugar
300ml, ½pt double cream, whipped

Stir the rosehip syrup into the apple purée. Beat the egg yolks and add the caster sugar. Whisk until pale and thick. Stir in the cream and the apple and rosehip purée. Beat the egg whites until stiff and fold them in gently until all is well mixed together. Freeze until firm.

ROWANBERRIES

These are the berries of the Mountain Ash. They are a beautiful deep orange colour and hang in clusters, ready to be picked from August to November. The Mountain Ash is a small tree with a grey bark and toothed leaves. The berries make an excellent jelly to eat with game, poultry or lamb.

ROWAN AND CRAB APPLE JELLY

Yield will vary depending on the juiciness of the fruit - 1kg or 2lb of sugar should yield 1.5kg or just over 3lb of jelly.

1kg, 2.2lb rowanberries
2kg, 4.4lb crab or cooking apples
granulated sugar

Cook the rowanberries and apples separately. The rowanberries need just enough water over the bottom of the saucepan to prevent them from burning. The apples should be cut up and barely covered with water. Cook both sets of fruit until soft and then strain through a muslin bag. Combine the juices and for every 600ml or 1pt of juice add 450g or 1lb of sugar. Gently heat until the sugar has dissolved and then boil rapidly until setting point is reached. Pot and cover. This makes a beautiful bright pink jelly and goes well with lamb.

ROWAN AND THYME JELLY

Yield will vary depending on the juiciness of the fruit - 1kg or 2lb of sugar should yield 1.5kg or just over 3lb of jelly.

1kg, 2.2lb rowanberries
300ml, ½pt water
granulated sugar
2 tbsp lemon juice
1tbsp chopped thyme to each 600ml or 1pt of juice

Wash the rowanberries and put in a large saucepan with the water. Bring to the boil and simmer until soft, crushing the berries on the side of the saucepan to help extract the juice. Strain through muslin overnight. Measure the liquid and for every 600ml or 1pt of liquid add 450g or 1lb of sugar, the lemon juice and chopped thyme. Over the heat allow the sugar to dissolve and then bring to a rapid boil. Boil until setting point is reached – this may take up to 25 minutes. Pour into warmed, sterilised jars and seal.

SLOES

Sloes are the dark berries of the blackthorn, a thorny shrub which grows wild throughout Europe and is also native to North Africa and Asia. The stones from sloes have been found on prehistoric sites so they have obviously been useful in the diet of Early Man. The sloe is the ancestor of all cultivated plums. These shrubs are most often found in the hedgerows, growing up to 3 metres high. They have long thorns and oval leaves and tiny white flowers appear before the leaves. The fruits resemble tiny plums and have blue-black skins. The juicy green flesh is very acid and can't be eaten raw. Sloes ripen in the autumn but are best picked after the first frosts as this softens the skin.

APPLE AND SLOE JELLY

Yield will vary depending on the juiciness of the fruit - 1kg or 2lb of sugar should yield 1.5kg or just over 3lb of jelly.

450g, 1lb sloes
900g, 2lb cooking apples, chopped
granulated sugar

Put the sloes and apples in a preserving pan and just cover with water. Cook until the fruit is soft, crushing the sloes against the side of the pan to release their juices. Strain overnight through muslin. Measure the liquid and for every 600ml or 1pt of liquid add 450g, or 1lb of sugar. Over the heat allow the sugar to dissolve and then bring to a rapid boil. Boil until setting point is reached – this may take up to 25 minutes. Pour into warmed, sterilised jars and seal.

SLOE AND APPLE CHEESE

Each 450g, 1lb of sugar used will yield 750g, 1lb 10oz of cheese.

1kg, 2.2lb sloes
1 kg, 2.2lb cooking apples, chopped (skins and cores
included)
water
granulated sugar

Put the sloes and apples, with just enough water to cover, in a saucepan and cook until the fruits are soft. Sieve them to remove skin and stones. Measure the purée and for every 600ml or 1pt of juice use 450g, or 1lb of sugar. Return the purée to the pan and add the sugar. Heat gently to dissolve the sugar and then bring to the boil. Turn down the heat and simmer, stirring every so often until the mixture is very thick. This might take up to an hour. Spoon into moulds and cover.

SLOE GIN

225g, 8oz sloes
125g, 5oz caster sugar
1 x 70cl bottle of cheap gin
few drops of almond essence

Prick the sloes with a fork and put into a 1 litre, 2 pint Kilner jar. Add the sugar and pour in the gin. Add the almond essence, cover and shake the jar well. Leave in a cool, dark place for at least three months. Give the jar a shake once a week. Then strain off the sloes (and

reserve for sloe chocolates on page 94). Pour the liqueur into a bottle and store until needed.

ICED SLOE GIN AND APPLE SOUFFLÉ
Serves 4 – 6

3 egg whites
60ml, 2fl oz water
175g, 6oz caster sugar
300ml, ½pt unsweetened apple purée
2 tbsp sloe gin
300ml, ½pt double cream, whipped

Whisk the egg whites until stiff. Dissolve the sugar in the water over a gentle heat and then boil for 3 minutes. Pour this sugar syrup onto the egg whites as you continue to whisk them and whisk until thick. Fold in the apple purée and the sloe gin. Lastly stir in the double cream. Spoon into a freezer container and freeze until firm.

SLOE BRANDY

225g, 8oz sloes
100g, 4oz honey + 2 peeled almonds
1 x 70cl bottle of brandy

Prick the sloes with a fork and put into a 1 litre, 2 pint
Kilner jar. Add the honey and almonds and fill up with
brandy. Leave for three months and strain before
drinking.

SLOE CHOCOLATES

225g, 8oz sloes which were used to make sloe gin
225g, 8oz milk chocolate

Remove the stones from the gin-soaked sloes. Melt
the chocolate and, using a fork, dip each sloe in some
chocolate to cover completely. Leave to set. This makes
a nice alcoholic treat.

CHESTNUTS

The sweet chestnut tree originated in the eastern Mediterranean – the Greeks introduced the trees into Europe. The word chestnut comes from the Greek 'Castanea', named after a city in ancient Asia Minor. The Romans cultivated them and brought them to Britain. These tall upright trees have long pointed serrated leaves and the fruits, usually three together, are enclosed in round green spiky cases. Trees can be found in parks and on the edges of woods. The nuts ripen in October/November and will fall off the tree – you can gather the nuts, prize them from their husks and then slit the brown shells before you cook them to prevent them from exploding. They cannot be eaten raw like other nuts. You can either boil, roast or grill them. They have a soft, floury texture and can be used in both sweet and savoury dishes. The Romans ground chestnuts into flour and the Italians used chestnut flour to make polenta before maize was introduced in the early 16th century. Nowadays Spain is the main exporter of the sweet or Spanish chestnut (castanea sativa).

Chestnuts are low in oil and are therefore lower in calories than other nuts but high in carbohydrates. They are a good source of potassium. Chestnuts are used to make marrons glaces which are crystallized.

CHESTNUT PURÉE

To make chestnut purée you must slit the shells and boil the chestnuts in water for 10 minutes. Allow to cool and then peel off the shells and inner skin. Simmer the nuts for a further 40 minutes in a little water and then drain and purée them in a food processor. To make sweetened purée make a sugar syrup using 350g, 12oz of granulated sugar to 600ml, 1pt of water. Dissolve the sugar in the water over a gentle heat, add 450g, 1lb of peeled chestnuts and a teaspoon of vanilla essence. Boil until the chestnuts are soft. Remove the chestnuts and mash them up, then mix in enough of the sugar syrup to make a soft consistency.

CHESTNUT SOUP
Serves 4 – 6

450g, 1lb chestnuts
1.2 litres, 2pts chicken stock
1 onion, peeled and chopped
50g, 2oz butter
salt and pepper
4 tbsp single cream

Cover the chestnuts with water in a saucepan and bring to the boil. Drain and peel them, then return to the saucepan and cook in the stock until tender. This will take at least 20 minutes. Put them in the food processor with a little of the cooking liquid and process them. Cook the onion in the butter until soft, add the chestnut mixture and some of the stock until you have the right consistency. Season and add the cream before serving.

BULGAR WHEAT SALAD WITH
CHESTNUTS AND BUTTERNUT SQUASH
Serves 4

3 red onions, peeled
half a butternut squash
6 tbsp olive oil
225g, 8oz bulgar wheat
600ml, 1pt vegetable stock
175g, 6oz cooked chestnuts
1 tbsp parsley
1 tbsp chives

Cut the onions into quarters and dice the butternut squash. Put into a roasting tin and drizzle with half the olive oil. Roast in the oven at gas mark 6, 200°C (400°F) for 25 minutes. Heat the rest of the oil in a saucepan and add the bulgar wheat. Then pour on the vegetable stock. Bring to the boil, then lower the heat and simmer for 15 minutes, by which time the stock should have been absorbed. Mix the chestnuts into the roasted onion and squash. Fold the vegetables into the bulgar wheat and add the herbs.

BRUSSELS SPROUTS WITH CHESTNUTS
Serves 4

450g, 1lb Brussels sprouts, peeled
225g, 8oz chestnuts, cooked
50g, 2oz butter
25g, 1oz brown breadcrumbs

Steam or boil the sprouts for 5 minutes. Warm the chestnuts in a pan in a little water. Melt the butter in a saucepan and toss in the sprouts and chestnuts. Stir through the breadcrumbs and transfer to a serving dish.

CHESTNUT STUFFING

225g, 8oz chestnuts, skinned
225g, 8oz unsmoked bacon, chopped
1 onion, peeled and chopped
1 tsp caster sugar
25g, 1oz butter
25g, 1oz porridge oats
75g, 3oz brown breadcrumbs
1 egg, beaten
salt and pepper

Cook the chestnuts in boiling water until soft. Drain and chop them up. Fry the bacon until the fat runs out and then add the onion and sugar. Cook until beginning to brown and then add the butter, oats, breadcrumbs and chestnuts. Allow the butter to melt, then turn off the heat and bind the mixture together with the egg, adding salt and pepper to taste. Use to stuff the turkey at Christmas.

CHESTNUT MOUSSE
Serves 4

2 eggs, separated
150ml, ¼pt milk
2 tsp powdered gelatine
2 tbsp water
225g, 8oz sweetened chestnut purée
150ml, ¼pt double cream, whipped

Put the egg yolks and milk into a bowl over a saucepan of gently simmering water. Stir until the mixture thickens and becomes custard like. Dissolve the gelatine in the water over a gentle heat. Beat into the chestnut purée with the custard. Stir in the double cream. Whisk the egg whites until stiff and fold them into the chestnut mixture. Spoon into a serving bowl and chill until set.

CHESTNUT AND ORANGE COMPOTE
Serves 4

450g, 1lb chestnuts
600ml, 1pt water
100g, 4oz granulated sugar
few drops of vanilla essence
3 oranges, peeled and cut into chunks

Put the chestnuts into a saucepan and cover with water. Bring to the boil and then drain and peel. Put the sugar and the water into a saucepan with the vanilla essence. Boil for 5 minutes, add the chestnuts and simmer gently for about an hour. Allow to cool. Add the oranges to the chestnuts in a serving bowl.

MONT BLANC
Serves 4

3 egg whites
175g, 6oz caster sugar
450g, 1lb chestnut purée, unsweetened
125g, 5oz icing sugar
1 tsp vanilla essence
1 tbsp brandy
150ml, ¼pt double cream, whipped

First make four meringue nests by whisking the egg whites until very stiff, then whisk in half the caster sugar. Fold in the rest of the sugar and place large spoonfuls on greased baking sheets, indenting them in the middle so that they look like nests. Bake in the oven at gas mark 1, 120°C (275°F) for an hour. Meanwhile mix or process together the chestnut purée, icing sugar, vanilla essence and brandy. Spoon some of this chestnut mixture into each meringue nest and top with a spoonful of cream.

CHOCOLATE AND CHESTNUT CAKE

75g, 3oz plain chocolate
2 tbsp water
4 eggs, separated
225g, 8oz caster sugar
300g, 12oz chestnuts, cooked and sieved

Filling

150ml, ¼pt double cream, whipped

Melt the chocolate with the water over a pan of simmering water. Add the egg yolks and sugar and whisk until thick. Whisk the egg whites and fold in with the chestnuts. Turn into a greased 20cm, 8in cake tin and cook at gas mark 4, 180°C (350°F) for 30 minutes. Turn out and when cool cut the cake into two halves. Sandwich together with whipped cream.

CHESTNUT GATEAU

50g, 2oz butter
50g, 2oz brown sugar
225g, 8oz unsweetened chestnut purée
1 tsp vanilla essence
3 eggs, separated

Cream together the butter and sugar and gradually beat in the chestnut purée and vanilla essence. Whisk the egg yolks until thick and stir into the mixture. Whisk the egg whites until stiff and fold them in. Spoon the mixture into a greased 20cm, 8in cake tin and bake for about 40 minutes at gas mark 4, 180°C (350°F). Leave to cool. When ready to serve, turn out and serve with cream.

HAZELNUTS

The hazel tree is probably the most widespread of nut trees in Britain. Other similar types are the filberts, which produce oval nuts and cobnuts which are round. Filberts were around in ancient times and the Romans probably brought them to Britain. Harvesting for filberts used to begin on 22 August, St Philbert's day. Hazels are shrubby trees found in woods, thickets and hedgerows with the familiar yellow catkins (also known as lambs' tails). These are the male flowers, which appear in January, and in order for the tree to bear fruit, the pollen from the catkins must reach the stigmas of the female flowers (sometimes called red ladies) which are tiny and red and look like a sea urchin. The problem is that the female flowers have to be pollinated by catkins from another hazel tree nearby and rely on the wind for pollination. The nuts, which are small and round and with thinner shells than commercially grown filberts and cobnuts grow in clusters of two or three, hanging down under a leaf. Before the First World War on Holy Cross Day which was 14 September, village schools used to close so that everyone could go nutting. The problem with gathering hazelnuts in the autumn

is that you have to get to them before the squirrels. If you pick them in late August when the nuts are still on the tree they may well not be good – too soft and likely to wither in their shells. It is best to wait for the nuts to fall in late September when they are ripe and brown. You will still be competing with the squirrels, birds and dormice (for which the nuts are a vital food source). If you are thinking of planting your own hazel trees you must wait seven years before nuts will be produced. Cobnuts are grown commercially mainly in orchards in Kent. Trees can yield up to 18 kg, 40lb of nuts. Hazelnuts are extremely rich in protein and calcium and are high in monounsaturated fat, the good fat that is said to lower cholesterol. They are also an excellent source of minerals such as potassium, phosphorus and magnesium.

FENNEL, APPLE AND HAZELNUT SALAD
Serves 4 – 6 as a side dish

2 small bulbs of fennel, sliced
4 red eating apples, cored and sliced finely
50g, 2oz hazelnuts, chopped
1 large carrot, peeled and grated
2 tbsp lemon juice
1 tbsp olive oil
150ml, ¼pt mayonnaise

Put the fennel, apple slices and hazelnuts in a bowl. Mix in the grated carrot. Sprinkle with the lemon juice and a little olive oil. Add the mayonnaise and stir everything together until the mayonnaise is evenly combined.

TURKEY WITH LEMON AND HAZELNUTS
Serves 4

4 turkey breast fillets
2 eggs, beaten
175g, 6oz hazelnuts, finely chopped
75g, 3oz butter

Sauce
120ml, 4 fl oz dry white vermouth
2 tbsp lemon juice
1 tbsp fresh tarragon, chopped
75g, 3oz butter, diced

Beat the turkey fillets with a rolling pin. Dip the turkey into the beaten egg. Spread the hazelnuts out on a plate and coat the fillets with them. Heat the butter in a large frying pan, add the turkey and fry for 5 minutes on each side, until golden brown. Remove and keep warm. To make the sauce add the vermouth to the pan and boil until reduced by half. Add the lemon juice, tarragon and seasoning. Off the heat whisk in the diced butter to thicken. Pour over the turkey and garnish with lemon.

SPAGHETTI WITH LEMON, NUTS AND HERBS
Serves 4

50g, 2oz butter
75g, 3oz hazelnuts, toasted and chopped
5 garlic cloves, peeled and chopped
grated rind and juice of 2 lemons
450g, 1lb spaghetti

handful of basil leaves
handful of parsley, chopped
2 tbsp single cream
salt and pepper

Melt the butter in a frying pan and add the hazelnuts and garlic. Fry for a minute, add the lemon rind and set aside. Cook the spaghetti according to the instructions on the packet. Drain and stir into the butter mixture. Add the herbs, lemon juice, cream and seasoning. Serve immediately.

OATMEAL AND HAZELNUT LOAF
Makes 1 loaf

100g, 4oz self-raising flour
¼ tsp bicarbonate of soda
50g, 2oz coarse oatmeal
75g, 3oz hazelnuts, chopped
2 tbsp olive oil
1 tbsp honey
1 egg
150ml, ¼pt soured cream

Sift the flour and bicarbonate of soda into a bowl. Add the oatmeal and hazelnuts and mix well. Put the oil, honey and egg into another bowl and beat with a whisk. Add the flour mixture and stir together until smooth. Stir in the soured cream. Spoon into a greased 450g, 1lb loaf tin and leave to rest for 10 minutes before baking in the oven at gas mark 4, 180°C (350°F) for 45 minutes. Leave in the tin to cool for a few minutes and then turn on to a wire rack to cool.

APPLE AND CARDAMOM WITH HAZELNUT CRUMBLE
Serves 4 - 6

675g, 1½lb cooking apples, peeled, cored and sliced
75g, 3oz granulated sugar
6 – 8 cardamom pods

Crumble

150g, 5oz plain flour
75g, 3oz soft brown sugar
100g, 4oz butter
50g, 2oz hazelnuts, chopped

Layer the apples in a baking dish and sprinkle with the granulated sugar. Extract the seeds from the cardamom pods and lightly crush them with a pestle and mortar. Add to the apples. Mix the flour with the brown sugar and rub in the butter. Stir in the hazelnuts and sprinkle over the apple mixture. Cook at gas mark 4, 180°C (350°F) for 30 minutes. Serve hot with cream.

GOOEY CHOCOLATE AND HAZELNUT PUDDING CAKE
Serves 6

This is a flourless cake, delicious with Greek yoghurt or cream, warm or cold.

175g, 6oz plain chocolate
100g, 4oz butter

3 eggs, separated
100g, 4oz light brown sugar
100g, 4oz hazelnuts, ground

Melt the chocolate and butter together and stir until smooth. Whisk together the egg yolks and brown sugar until thick and creamy. Stir in the chocolate mixture and fold in the hazelnuts. Whisk the egg whites and carefully hold them it. Spoon into a greased 20cm, 8in deep flan dish and bake in the oven at gas mark 4, 180°C (350°F) for about 40 minutes or until a skewer stuck in the centre comes out clean.

HAZELNUT AND MUSCOVADO MERINGUES
Makes 18

3 egg whites
175g, 6oz light muscovado sugar
25g, 1oz hazelnuts, finely chopped

Whisk the egg whites until really stiff. Whisk in the sugar a tablespoon at a time. You should have a thick meringue mixture. Put spoonfuls on to greased baking sheets and sprinkle the nuts evenly over the meringues. Bake at gas mark ¼, 110°C (225°F) for 2 hours. Leave to cool in the oven.

HAZELNUT AND CHOCOLATE
MERINGUE CAKE
Serves 6 - 8

4 egg whites
225g, 8oz caster sugar
1 tsp white wine vinegar
1 tsp vanilla essence
100g, 4oz ground hazelnuts

Filling
210ml, 7fl oz double cream, whipped
75g, 3oz plain chocolate, grated

Whisk the egg whites until very stiff. Whisk in the sugar, a tablespoon at a time until all is incorporated. Add the vinegar and vanilla essence and fold in the ground hazelnuts using a metal spoon. Spread the meringue in two equal circles about 20cm, 8in in diameter on two greased baking sheets. Cook in the oven at gas mark 4, 180°C (350°F) for about 35 minutes. The meringue circles may crack and crumble a little when you turn them out. Fold the grated chocolate into the cream and sandwich between the layers of meringue.

HAZELNUT DROPS
Makes about 20

2 large egg whites
25g, 1oz ground rice

100g, 4oz ground hazelnuts
225g, 8oz caster sugar

Beat the egg whites with the ground rice, hazelnuts and sugar for a couple of minutes. Leave to stand for a few minutes. Then drop small spoonfuls on to greased baking sheets and bake in the oven for 20 minutes at gas mark 4, 180°C (350°F).

HAZELNUT ICE CREAM
Serves 6 - 8
This goes well with blackcurrant or blackberry sauce.

175g, 6oz granulated sugar
120ml, 4 fl oz water
5 egg yolks
300ml, ½pt double cream, whipped
75g, 3oz hazelnuts, toasted and ground

Combine the sugar and water in a saucepan and heat gently until the sugar dissolves. Boil for 5 minutes. Beat the egg yolks until thick and continue to whisk as you pour in the sugar syrup. Whisk until cooled and then fold in the double cream and the hazelnuts. Pour into a freezer container and freeze.

LEMON AND HAZELNUT ROULADE
WITH CHOCOLATE CREAM
Serves 8

For the roulade

5 eggs, separated
125g, 5oz caster sugar
grated rind and juice of 1 lemon
50g, 2oz ground hazelnuts

For the filling

300ml, ½pt double cream
75g, 3oz dark chocolate, grated
50g, 2oz white chocolate, grated
50g, 2oz chopped hazelnuts for sprinkling

Line a Swiss roll tin with greaseproof paper. To make the roulade, whisk the egg yolks in a bowl, gradually adding the caster sugar and whisking until the mixture is pale and thick. Whisk in the lemon juice and fold in the ground hazelnuts and grated lemon rind. Whisk the egg whites until stiff and fold them into the lemon mixture. Pour into the Swiss roll tin. Bake in the oven at gas mark 4, 180°C (350°F) for about 20 minutes. Take out the roulade and cover with a damp tea towel. Leave for a few hours. To make the filling, whip the cream until thick but not too stiff. Fold in the grated chocolate. Place a piece of greaseproof paper on your work surface and cover with icing sugar. Tip the roulade out onto the icing sugar. Carefully peel off the lining

paper. Spread the cream over the roulade and roll up. Don't worry if it splits in places. This is quite normal. Dust with more icing sugar and sprinkle with hazelnuts before serving.

HONEY AND HAZELNUT MUFFINS
Makes 12 muffins

175g, 6oz plain flour
1 tsp baking power
175g, 6oz porridge oats
½ tsp bicarbonate of soda
175g, 6oz plain yoghurt
125g, 5oz honey
1½ tsp vanilla essence
1 large egg
4 tbsp vegetable oil
225g, 8oz roasted hazelnuts, chopped

Combine the first four dry ingredients. Whisk together all the wet ingredients. Mix the wet ingredients into the dry ingredients. Fold in the hazelnuts. The batter will be slightly lumpy. Pour into muffin tins and bake in the oven at gas mark 6, 200°C (400°F) for 20 minutes.

LEMON AND LIME SHORTBREAD
WITH HAZELNUTS
Makes about 15 slices

100g, 4oz butter
50g, 2oz caster sugar
¼ tsp finely grated lemon rind
¼ tsp finely grated lime rind
100g, 4oz plain flour
50g, 2oz cornflour
50g, 2oz hazelnuts, finely chopped

Put the butter and sugar in a food processor and whiz to combine. Add the grated rinds and the flours and process until the mixture comes together. Add the hazelnuts and process briefly. Press the mixture into a greased 20cm, 8in square cake tin and bake in the oven at gas mark 3, 160°C (325°F) for 20 minutes, until pale brown. Leave to cool before cutting into slices.

HAZELNUT AND CHOCOLATE COOKIES
Makes about 12 – 16 biscuits

50g, 2oz butter
100g, 4oz light muscovado sugar
1 egg yolk
75g, 3oz plain flour
50g, 2oz hazelnuts, roasted and ground
50g, 2oz plain chocolate, chopped into small pieces

Cream together the butter and sugar. Mix in the egg yolk. Gradually stir in the flour and hazelnuts and mix

in the chocolate. Form the mixture into small balls and place on greased baking sheets, flattening them slightly. Give them room to spread a little. Bake in the oven for about 15 minutes at gas mark 4, 180°C (350°F). Remove and allow to cool before transferring to a plate.

HAZELNUT AND WHITE
CHOCOLATE BLONDIES
Makes 18 squares

75g, 3oz butter
200g, 7oz demerara sugar
125g, 5oz plain flour
1 tsp baking powder
2 eggs, beaten
1 tsp vanilla essence
50g, 2oz hazelnuts, chopped
50g, 2oz white chocolate, cut into small chunks

Melt the butter and demerara sugar together and allow to cool. Sift the flour with the baking powder. Mix together the eggs and vanilla essence and stir in the butter and sugar mixture. Add the sifted flour and mix to combine. Lastly fold in the nuts and chocolate. Pour the mixture into a greased 27.5cm x 17.5cm (11 x 7in) tin and bake for 25 minutes in the oven at gas mark 4, 180°C (350°F). Leave to cool in the tin and cut into squares.

HAZELNUT AND CHOCOLATE FINGERS
Makes 15 slices

100g, 4oz butter
150g, 5oz plain chocolate
1 tbsp golden syrup
175g, 6oz digestive biscuits, crushed
75g, 3oz hazelnuts, ground

Melt the butter, chocolate and golden syrup together. Mix in the crushed biscuits and hazelnuts. When everything is thoroughly mixed together, press the mixture into a greased 20cm, 8in square tin and smooth the top. Refrigerate for 30 minutes and then cut into slices.

CARROT AND HAZELNUT CAKE
Serves 8

200g, 7oz self-raising flour
½ tsp ground ginger
½ tsp ground cinnamon
75g, 3oz light muscovado sugar
50g, 2oz hazelnuts, finely chopped
100g, 4oz carrots, peeled and grated
120ml, 4fl oz sunflower oil
2 small eggs, beaten
grated rind and juice of 1 lemon

Icing
100g, 4oz cream cheese
50g, 2oz butter
50g, 2oz icing sugar

Sift the flour with the ginger and cinnamon. Mix in the sugar, hazelnuts and carrot. Stir in the oil, eggs and grated rind and juice from the lemon. Spoon into a greased 20cm, 8in round cake tin. Cook in the oven at gas mark 4, 180°C (350°F) for 30 minutes. Cool the cake and slice through the middle to make two rounds. To make the filling beat together the cream cheese, butter and icing sugar and use to sandwich the two cakes together.

HAZELNUT AND COFFEE CAKE
Serves 8

175g, 6oz butter
175g, 6oz caster sugar
175g, 6oz self-raising flour
50g, 2oz hazelnuts, coarsely ground
1 tsp baking powder
3 eggs
3 tsp coffee essence

Icing
275g, 10oz icing sugar
75g, 3oz butter
2 tsp coffee essence
50g, 2oz hazelnuts, chopped

Mix all the cake ingredients together in a large bowl or in a food processor. Spoon into 2 greased 20cm, 8in round cake tins and spread evenly. Bake at gas mark 3, 170°C (325°F) for 40 minutes. Cool. To make the icing beat the icing sugar into the butter and add the coffee essence. Use half the icing to sandwich the cakes together. Mix the nuts into the remaining icing and spread over the top of the cake.

WALNUTS

He who plants a walnut tree expects not to eat of
the fruit.
Walnuts and Pears you plant for your heirs.
A Woman, a Dog, and a Walnut Tree, the more you
beat them the better they be.

Walnut trees are native to Western Asia and were very
popular with the Greeks and Romans. The Greeks used
to dedicate them to Artemis. They were only introduced
into Britain five hundred years ago. Walnut trees are
slow-growing but make huge trees and can be found
scattered on the perimeter of old woods and parks. The
leaves and husks have been used as brown dyes and
the oil used as a hair darkener or for paints. Walnut
wood was much prized in the past and for this reason
walnut trees growing in the wild are quite hard to find.

Young walnuts can be picked in July and pickled in
their green outer covering. Otherwise walnuts are ready
for harvesting in October/November. You have to get
rid of the green outer husk and the inner shell. When
you peel off the husk, unless you wear gloves, you
hands will be stained yellow.

Walnuts are very nutritious and despite being high in
calories are very good for you. Walnuts are unique
because they contain omega 3 and omega 6
polyunsaturated fatty acids. These essential fatty acids
reduce the risk of heart disease by helping to lower
harmful cholesterol. They are a valuable source of
phosphorus but only the husk contains vitamin C.

PICKLED WALNUTS

Green walnuts (picked in July)
salt
water
pickling vinegar

Make up a brine using 175g, 6oz salt to 1 litre, 2 pints of water. Wear gloves and prick the walnuts with a skewer. Put the walnuts in the brine and make up a fresh solution of brine every day for a week. Remove the walnuts and dry in a sunny place until they go black. Then pack them in jars covering them with hot pickling vinegar. Seal the jars and leave for a month before trying them.

WALNUT AND POMEGRANATE DIP
Makes 2 small bowls

175g, 6oz walnuts, toasted
350g, 12oz roasted red peppers, drained
4 tbsp olive oil
1 tbsp pomegranate molasses
2 cloves of garlic, peeled
½ tsp ground cumin
½ tsp dried chilli flakes

Combine all the ingredients in a food processor and process until smooth. Chill for at least an hour before serving as a dip with cut up vegetables such as carrots and cucumbers.

MACKEREL AND WALNUT PATÉ
Serves 6

*450g, 1lb fresh mackerel grilled, skin and bones
removed
1 clove of garlic, peeled and crushed
grated rind and juice of 1 lemon
225g, 8oz medium fat cream cheese
1 tbsp fresh chives, chopped
50g, 2oz walnuts, toasted and broken into small bits*

Put the mackerel in a food processor, add the garlic, lemon juice and rind and process. Add the cream cheese and chives and process again. Lastly fold in the walnuts.

WALNUT CHEESE

*75g, 3oz cream cheese
50g, 2oz mature Cheddar cheese, grated
few drops of Worcestershire sauce
50g, 2oz walnuts, chopped*

Beat the cream cheese and stir in the grated Cheddar cheese. Add the Worcestershire sauce and most of the walnuts, keeping a few for decoration. Press the mixture into a mould or ramekin dish. When ready to serve turn out and decorate with the reserved walnuts.

MUSHROOM AND WALNUT SOUP
Serves 6

50g, 2oz butter
1 onion, peeled and finely chopped
350g, 12oz mushrooms, chopped
1 tbsp plain flour
600ml, 1pt vegetable stock
300ml, ½pt milk
75g, 3oz walnuts, chopped
salt and pepper to taste
150ml, ¼pt single cream
croutons

Melt the butter in a saucepan and gently fry the onion and chopped mushrooms. Stir in the flour and then the stock, milk and walnuts. Season to taste. Stir until smooth and then bring to the boil. Lower the heat, cover and simmer for about 30 minutes. Purée the soup, add the cream and gently reheat, without boiling. Serve with croutons.

WALNUT, PEAR AND
FETA CHEESE SALAD
Serves 2 - 3

1 head of endive
2 pears, cored and sliced
1 avocado, peeled and sliced
2 tsp lemon juice
100g, 4oz Feta cheese
50g, 2oz walnuts, chopped
3 tbsp olive oil
1 tbsp white wine vinegar
pinch of sugar, salt and pepper to taste

Tear the endive into separate leaves and scatter in a serving bowl. Arrange the pear slices and avocado over the endive and sprinkle with lemon juice. Crumble the Feta cheese and scatter with the walnuts over the salad. Make a vinaigrette by mixing the vinegar into the olive oil. Add the pinch of sugar, salt and pepper. Pour over the salad and serve.

CHICKEN AND WALNUT SALAD
Serves 4

1 head Cos lettuce, shredded or torn into pieces
450g, 1lb cooked chicken, diced
75g, 3oz walnuts, chopped
2 green eating apples, cored and sliced
1 red pepper, deseeded and diced
2 tbsp lemon juice

180ml, 6fl oz mayonnaise
1 tbsp fresh chives, chopped

Combine the lettuce, chicken, walnuts, sliced apples and diced pepper. Sprinkle with lemon juice and stir in the mayonnaise. Sprinkle with chives and serve.

POTATO, EGG AND WALNUT SALAD
Serves 4

450g, 1lb new potatoes, boiled with skins
2 eggs, boiled and sliced
50g, 2oz walnuts, chopped
1 tbsp fresh chives, chopped

Dressing

6 tbsp olive oil
1½ tbsp white wine vinegar
pinch of sugar
salt and pepper

Slice the boiled potatoes and arrange in a serving bowl. Scatter the sliced eggs, walnuts and chives over the top. To make the dressing mix together the oil and vinegar and add a pinch of sugar, salt and pepper to taste. Pour over the potato salad and serve while the potatoes are still warm.

RED CABBAGE WITH
BACON AND WALNUTS
Serves 3 - 4 as a side dish

1 small red cabbage
100g, 4oz unsmoked streaky bacon
2 tbsp olive oil
3 tbsp white wine vinegar
1 tsp granulated sugar
1 tsp Dijon mustard
squeeze of lemon juice
75g, 3oz walnuts

Halve the cabbage, cut out the central core and any damaged outer leaves. Shred finely and put in a steamer. Steam for 5 minutes. In the meantime cut the bacon into small pieces and in a frying pan sauté the bacon without any oil until crisp. Add the bacon to the cabbage in a serving bowl. Add the olive oil to the frying pan and stir in the vinegar, sugar, mustard and squeeze of lemon juice. Increase the heat and boil for a minute or so, adding the walnuts to heat them through. Pour the hot dressing and walnuts over the cabbage and serve at once.

TAGLIETELLE WITH
WALNUTS AND CREAM
Serves 4

450g, 1lb taglietelle
50g, 2oz butter
1 clove of garlic, peeled and chopped
175g, 6oz walnuts, chopped
175g, 6oz cream cheese
50g, 2oz Parmesan or Cheddar cheese, grated
1 tbsp parsley, chopped

Cook the taglietelle according to the instructions on the packet. Meanwhile melt the butter and add the garlic and walnuts. Cook for 3 minutes. Add the cream cheese and stir until smooth. Drain the pasta, add the grated Parmesan or Cheddar cheese and stir in the cream cheese sauce. Scatter the parsley over the pasta and serve immediately.

LEMONY CHICKEN AND LEEKS WITH BREADCRUMB TOPPING
Serves 4

125g, 5oz butter
450g, 1lb leeks, sliced
50g, 2oz plain flour
600ml, 1pt chicken stock
150ml, ¼pt milk
2 tbsp lemon juice
450g, 1lb cooked chicken, chopped
100g, 4oz wholemeal bread
2 garlic cloves, peeled and crushed
50g, 2oz walnuts, toasted and chopped
sprig of oregano, chopped

Melt 50g, 2oz of the butter in a frying pan and fry the leeks for a few minutes. Stir in the flour and cook for a couple of minutes, stirring. Then gradually add the chicken stock and milk. Bring to the boil and simmer for a few minutes. Season and add the lemon juice. Stir the chicken into the sauce and spoon into an ovenproof dish. Melt the remaining butter. Crumble the bread and mix into the butter along with the garlic, walnuts and oregano. Sprinkle over the chicken and cook in the oven at gas mark 6, 200°C (400°F) for 20 minutes.

WALNUT AND CHEESE STRAWS

100g, 4oz butter
175g, 6oz plain flour
50g, 2oz Parmesan cheese, grated
50g, 2oz walnuts, finely chopped
1 egg yolk
1 tbsp cold water

Rub the butter into the flour until finely blended. Add the cheese and nuts. Bind together with the egg yolk and water. Then roll out and cut into strips. Place on greased baking sheets and bake in the oven at gas mark 4, 180°C (350°F) for 10 – 15 minutes.

ROSEMARY BUTTERED WALNUTS

225g, 8oz walnut halves
50g, 2oz butter
1 tbsp olive oil
1 tbsp fresh rosemary, chopped
½ tsp salt
½ tsp hot paprika

Melt the butter and olive oil in a frying pan and add the walnuts. Fry turning over frequently, adding the rosemary, salt and paprika after a couple of minutes. When browned all over, drain on kitchen paper and serve straightaway.

WALNUT, APPLE AND CHEESE BREAD
Makes 1 loaf

25g, 1oz butter
225g, 8oz self-raising flour
1 eating apple, peeled, cored and grated
50g, 2oz walnuts, chopped
75g, 3oz mature Cheddar cheese, grated
1 egg
150ml, ¼pt milk

Rub the butter into the flour and add the apple, walnuts and cheese. Stir to combine and then add the egg and milk and bind together. Spoon into a greased 450g, 1lb loaf tin and bake in the oven at gas mark 5, 190°C (375°F) for 40 minutes until well risen and brown.

STICKY CHOCOLATE AND WALNUT PUDDING

Fudge Sauce
50g, 2oz butter
75g, 3oz brown sugar
150ml, ¼pt single cream

100g, 4oz dates, chopped
120ml, 4 fl oz boiling water
½ tsp bicarbonate of soda
75g, 3oz butter
50g, 2oz brown sugar
1 egg
100g, 4oz self-raising flour

1 tbsp cocoa powder
75g, 3oz walnuts, chopped

First make the fudge sauce. Heat the butter and sugar together in a saucepan and stir in the cream. Allow to boil for a couple of minutes. Use half this sauce to cover the bottom of a greased baking dish. Pour the boiling water over the dates and add the bicarbonate of soda. Allow to stand for a few minutes. Meanwhile cream the butter and sugar together and beat in the egg. Sift the flour and cocoa together and gradually incorporate the flour, walnuts and dates with their liquid into the mixture. Stir together until evenly combined and spoon over the fudge sauce. Cook in the oven at gas mark 4, 180°C (350°F) for about 30 minutes or until the sponge is cooked through. Serve with the rest of the fudge sauce, either poured over the top or served separately.

WALNUT BRANDY BUTTER
Packs into two small ramekins

175g, 6oz butter
75g, 3oz light muscovado sugar
1 tsp lemon juice
½ tbsp brandy
50g, 2oz walnuts, finely chopped

Beat together the butter, sugar, lemon juice and brandy. Fold in the walnuts until evenly distributed. Pack into a couple of small bowls and serve with Christmas pudding or mince pies.

TOFFEE WALNUT TART

175g, 6oz shortcrust pastry
225g, 8oz walnuts, roughly chopped
4 eggs, beaten
4 tbsp golden syrup
75g, 3oz butter
100g, 4oz brown sugar

Roll out the pastry and line a greased 20cm, 8in flan dish. Prick and bake blind in the oven at gas mark 4, 180°C (350°F) for 15 minutes. Allow to cool. Scatter the walnuts over the base. Put the eggs, golden syrup, butter and brown sugar in a bowl and place over a pan of simmering water. Stir, allowing the butter to melt and when evenly combined pour over the nuts. Bake in the oven at gas mark 4, 180°C (350°F) for about 25 minutes or until the filling is just set.

WALNUT AND APPLE TART
Serves 6 - 8

225g, 8oz shortcrust pastry
450g, 1lb cooking apples, peeled and cored
150ml, ¼pt whipping cream
100g, 4oz caster sugar
1 egg
75g, 3oz plain flour
1 tsp vanilla essence
1 tsp cinnamon
¼ tsp nutmeg
75g, 3oz walnuts, chopped

Line a greased 22.5cm, 9in flan dish with the pastry. Slice the apples and transfer to the flan dish. Mix together the cream, sugar, egg, flour, vanilla essence and spices (this can be done in a food processor if you have one). Pour over apple slices and top with the walnuts. Bake at gas mark 4, 180°C (350°F) for 40 minutes.

MAPLE AND WALNUT PRALINE ICE CREAM

For the praline
100g, 4oz granulated sugar
50g, 2oz walnuts

4 eggs, separated
150ml, ¼pt maple syrup
300ml, ½pt double cream, whipped

To make the praline put the sugar and walnuts in a heavy based pan and heat until the sugar turns to liquid. Do not stir but tilt the pan backwards and forwards to distribute the sugar evenly. Remove from the heat and pour the mixture on to a greased baking tin to harden. Crush to a powder with a rolling pin. Whisk the egg yolks with warmed maple syrup until thick. Stir into the cream. Whisk the egg whites and fold in with the praline. Pour into a freezer container and freeze until firm.

BLACK TREACLE AND WALNUT BREAD
Makes 1 large loaf

450g, 1lb plain flour
4 tsp baking powder
50g, 2oz soft brown sugar
100g, 4oz walnuts, chopped
3 tbsp black treacle, warmed
1 egg, beaten
120ml, 4fl oz milk

Sieve the flour with the baking powder. Add the sugar and walnuts. Mix in the treacle, egg and milk. Grease a 1kg, 2lb loaf tin and fill with the mixture. Leave to stand in a warm place for 20 minutes and then bake in the oven for 1 hour at gas mark 4, 180°C (350°F).

WALNUT MOCHA BROWNIES
Makes 16 squares

2 eggs
150g, 5oz dark muscovado sugar
100g, 4oz plain chocolate
100g, 4oz butter
1 tbsp liquid espresso coffee
75g, 3oz self-raising flour
50g, 2oz walnuts, chopped

Whisk the eggs and gradually add the muscovado sugar, trying to break up any lumps or hard bits. Melt together the chocolate, butter and coffee and stir into the egg mixture. Sieve the flour over the mixture and stir to

combine. Lastly add the walnuts. Pour the mixture into a greased 20cm, 8in square cake tin. Bake in the oven at gas mark 4, 180°C (350°F) for 30 minutes. Allow to cool before cutting into squares.

COFFEE AND WALNUT SWISS ROLL

3 eggs
75g, 3oz caster sugar
75g, 3oz self-raising flour
1 tbsp coffee essence
50g, 2oz walnuts, ground

Filling
150ml, ¼pt double cream
25g, 1oz icing sugar
1 tbsp coffee essence

Whisk together the eggs and caster sugar until pale and thick. Sieve the flour over the egg mixture and fold it in along with the coffee essence and walnuts quickly but carefully. Turn into a lined and greased Swiss roll tin and bake in the oven at gas mark 6, 200°C (400°F) for 10 minutes. Dampen a tea towel with hot water and lay out on the work surface. Lay a piece of greaseproof paper over the tea towel and sprinkle with caster sugar. Turn the Swiss roll out on to the greaseproof paper and carefully roll up with the lining paper inside. Allow to cool while you whip the cream with the icing sugar and coffee essence. Unroll and spread the coffee cream over the walnut sponge before rolling up again. Sprinkle with icing sugar before serving.

LIGHT WALNUT SPONGE WITH BUTTERSCOTCH CREAM

3 eggs, separated
100g, 4oz light brown sugar
125g, 5oz walnuts, toasted and ground
1 tbsp white breadcrumbs

Filling

50g, 2oz butter
125g, 5oz icing sugar
1 tbsp single cream

Whisk the egg yolks and brown sugar together until thick. Fold in the walnuts and breadcrumbs. Whisk the egg whites until stiff and gently fold them into the cake mixture. Divide the mixture between two greased 17.5cm, 7in cake tins and bake in the oven at gas mark 4, 180°C (350°F) for 15 minutes or until browned on top. To make the filling melt the butter in a saucepan and cook until the butter turns brown. Remove from the heat and stir into the icing sugar. Add the single cream and beat together until smooth. Use this butterscotch cream to sandwich the two halves of cake together.

WALNUT AND LEMON CAKE

75g, 3oz butter
150g, 5oz caster sugar
2 eggs
150g, 5oz self-raising flour
grated rind and juice of 1 lemon
1 tbsp poppy seeds
50g, 2oz walnuts, chopped

Topping

150g, 5oz icing sugar
1 tbsp Greek yoghurt
grated rind of ½ a lemon

You can mix all the ingredients except the walnuts together in a food processor or in a large bowl. When everything is well combined, add the walnuts and stir through the mixture. Spoon into a greased 17.5cm, 7in round cake tin and cook in the oven at gas mark 4, 180°C (350°F) for 20 – 25 minutes or until a skewer stuck in the cake comes out clean. Allow to cool and turn out on to a plate. To make the topping beat the icing sugar into the yoghurt and stir in the grated lemon rind. Spread over the top of the cake and put in the fridge so the yoghurt topping sets.

WALNUT AND BLUEBERRY
CHOCOLATE SLICES
Makes 15 slices

These are great for lunch boxes. You could leave out the topping. The walnuts, blueberries and oats makes these slices a nutritious snack.

50g, 2oz butter
75g, 3oz dark brown sugar
1 egg yolk
50g, 2oz plain flour
75g, 3oz porridge oats
1 tbsp golden syrup
50g, 2oz walnuts, chopped
1 tbsp dried blueberries

Topping

75g, 3oz plain chocolate
25g, 1oz butter

Beat together the butter and sugar. Stir in the egg yolk and mix in the flour, oats and golden syrup. Lastly add the walnuts and blueberries and make sure they are evenly combined before spreading the mixture out in a greased 20cm, 8in square tin. Bake in the oven at gas mark 4, 180°C (350°F) for 15 to 20 minutes. Remove and allow to cool slightly. Melt the chocolate and butter together and spread evenly over the oat mixture. When the chocolate topping is set cut into bars.

WALNUT AND CHOCOLATE COOKIES

75g, 3oz butter
175g, 6oz soft brown sugar
1 egg
2 tsp vanilla essence
175g, 6oz self-raising flour
50g, 2oz walnuts, chopped
75g, 3oz plain chocolate, chopped into small pieces

Cream the butter and sugar together. Beat in the egg and add the vanilla essence. Stir in the flour and mix in the walnuts and chocolate. Put spoonfuls on to greased baking sheets and flatten slightly. Leave room for them to spread. Cook for 10 minutes in the oven at gas mark 4, 180°C (350°F).

FUDGE-COATED WALNUTS

180ml, 6fl oz can evaporated milk
25g, 1oz butter
350g, 12oz granulated sugar
½ tsp vanilla essence
100g, 4oz walnuts

Put the evaporated milk, butter and granulated sugar in a saucepan and heat slowly until the sugar has dissolved. Bring to the boil and then lower slightly and allow to bubble away until the mixture registers 116°C (240°F) on a sugar thermometer or until a little dropped into a cup of cold water forms a soft ball. This should take 10 to 15 minutes. Beat in the vanilla essence and lastly mix in the walnuts stirring to coat evenly. Drop small spoonfuls on to greased baking sheets and allow to cool. Store in an airtight container.

POPPY SEEDS

It is likely that the Romans knew about poppies because Ceres, the corn goddess, is depicted with a bunch of poppies in her hand. The common field or corn poppy used to be more abundant than it is nowadays, especially in arable fields. Poppies can still be found mainly in the South of England in fields and wastelands but also along roadsides, hedgerows and in gardens. Poppies flower from June to September, at which time the petals fall off and the seed heads start to dry. The seed heads are the shape of an inverted cone. They are ready for picking when they are grey brown in colour and you will be able to see small holes just below the flat top. These are the holes from which the seeds would usually escape. Pick these heads, turn them upside down and you should be able to shake most of the seeds out into a paper bag or small container. Poppy seeds are very popular in Eastern European cooking, in particular in Slovakia, Romania, and the Middle East. In Britain we use them in bread, pastries, cakes and biscuits but also in salad dressings and sometimes in pasta dishes.

TAGLIETELLE WITH POPPY SEEDS
Serves 3 – 4

350g, 12oz taglietelle
50g, 2oz butter, melted
1 tbsp poppy seeds
1 tbsp fresh parsley, chopped
150ml, ¼pt soured cream
75g, 3oz Parmesan cheese, grated

Cook the taglietelle according to the packet instructions. Drain, return to the saucepan and keep warm over a low heat. Stir in the butter, poppy seeds, parsley and soured cream. Serve at once sprinkled with the Parmesan.

CARROT AND KALE WITH POPPY SEEDS
Serves 4

450g, 1lb carrots, scrubbed and sliced into sticks
bunch of curly kale, leaves separated
15g, ½oz butter
1 tbsp poppy seeds

Cook the carrots in salted water for between 5 and 8 minutes. Steam the kale for 3 or 4 minutes. Mix together in a serving dish with the butter. Sprinkle with poppy seeds and serve.

POPPY SEED DRESSING

This goes well with most salad leaves but especially rocket. It's also nice with a potato salad.

6 tbsp sunflower oil
2 tbsp balsamic vinegar
¼ tsp dry mustard
1 clove of garlic, peeled and crushed
pinch of sugar
1 tsp poppy seeds
salt and pepper to taste

Whisk together the oil and vinegar and stir in the mustard, garlic, sugar, poppy seeds, salt and pepper.

CHEESY POPPY SEED NIBBLES
Makes 30 small rounds

75g, 3oz wholemeal flour
50g, 2oz butter
1 tbsp poppy seeds
75g, 3oz Parmesan cheese, grated

Rub the butter into the flour until it resembles breadcrumbs. Mix in the poppy seeds and cheese. Bind together to form a dough. Chill for 10 minutes and then roll out until quite thin and cut into small rounds. Lay on greased baking sheets and bake in the oven at gas mark 4, 180°C (350°F) for 10 minutes.

POPPY SEED AND LEMON DRIZZLE LOAF
Makes a 450g, 1lb loaf

100g, 4oz butter
175g, 6oz caster sugar
2 eggs
175g, self-raising flour
1 tsp baking power
Grated rind of 1 lemon
4 tbsp milk
1 tbsp of poppy seeds
4 tbsp granulated sugar
juice of 1 lemon

Put the butter, caster sugar, eggs, flour and baking powder in a food processor and whiz until smooth. Add the grated lemon rind, milk and poppy seeds and whiz for another minute. Grease a 450g, 1lb loaf tin and pour the mixture in, spreading it out evenly. Bake in the oven at gas mark 4, 180°C (350°F) for 30 minutes or until a skewer inserted in the cake comes out clean. Meanwhile dissolve the granulated sugar in the lemon juice. Prick the loaf all over with the skewer and pour the sweetened lemon juice over the top of the loaf. Leave to cool completely before turning out of the tin.

POPPY SEED SHORTBREAD
Makes 8 slices

175g, 6oz plain flour
100g, 4oz butter
50g, 2oz caster sugar
2 tbsp poppy seeds

Place all the ingredients in a food processor and process until the mixture binds together. Chill for about 30 minutes and then press into a greased 23cm, 9in flan tin. Prick all over with a fork, sprinkle with a little more caster sugar and bake in the oven at gas mark 4, 180°C (350°F) for about 20 minutes or until pale brown.

Index

142